Financial Privacy & Electronic Commerce

Financial Privacy & Electronic Commerce

Who's In My Business

Benjamin E. Robinson III, Ph.D

Writers Club Press

San Jose New York Lincoln Shanghai

Financial Privacy & Electronic Commerce
Who's In My Business

Writers Club Press
an imprint of iUniverse.com, Inc.

For information address:
iUniverse.com, Inc.
620 North 48th Street, Suite 201
Lincoln, NE 68504-3467
www.iuniverse.com

ISBN: 0-595-13046-1

Printed in the United States of America

For Sydney, Bailey, and Ceci

Dedication and Acknowledgments

Foremost, I dedicate this book to Ceci, Sydney and Bailey. My family is my life and inspiration for anything I do in this world.

Professor José H. Cedillos served as my mentor. His experience in life, masterful outlook, and his personal support were the foundations for this study. Professor Clyde D. McKee, Jr. served as the catalyst for me to strive for the highest level of scholarship. He has always challenged me to examine and analyze my ideas for the social good. Mr. Edmund D. Cook, Jr., Esquire of Winston & Strawn guided me through the field of study. As a recognized expert in the field of public policy, he served as my role model. I am especially grateful for the assistance of Drs. Charles R. Howard and Barbara Trzcinski, for their unconditional support and encouragement throughout the study.

I want to express my warm gratitude to Professor Halloway C. Sells, who reviewed the manuscript for this project and provided a critical analysis. I also appreciate the resources of the Coalition of Service Industries and Privacy & American Business.

Finally, I thank Danyelle Williams for her resourcefulness and dedication to this study as an invaluable editor.

Benjamin E. Robinson III, Ph.D.
Norwalk, Connecticut

CONTENTS

Introduction 1
Part One 3
European Data Protection 3
Part Two 12
United States Privacy Policy 12
Part Three 28
Financial Sector Privacy 28
Part Four 38
Consumer Perceptions of Financial Privacy 38
Appendix A 57
Appendix B 59
Appendix C 61
Appendix D 65
Appendix E 67
Appendix F 71
Bibliography 123
About The Author 129

INTRODUCTION

The financial services sector has had a respectable track record in the protection of consumer privacy. However, business practices, industry consolidation, electronic commerce, and economic trends have raised consumer privacy as a key issue in the financial services sector. This is evidenced by the litany of articles and journals that are analyzing the recent phenomenon. For example, the *Privacy Journal, Privacy Times* and the Brookings Institute have dedicated significant resources on the issue of privacy and the financial services sector. Many new services have been developed for businesses to evaluate internal privacy procedures. Companies such as IBM have invented software packages to analyze privacy compliance efforts by corporations. Most major accounting firms have established privacy consulting sections to manage the increased demand.

Improvements in the rapid transfer of information provide a new medium for the purchase of goods and services, that is, the medium of electronic commerce. The European Union has forced the issue with the Data Protection Directive. As a result, the United States has had to debate the lack of regulation or standards governing the new medium of electronic commerce. The debate could hinder any advance by society to engage in new technology. Because of increased government attention through regulatory and legislative action, corporations are developing self-regulatory initiatives to create industry standards for electronic commerce. Recently, the Federal Trade Commission audited random Web sites to determine the level of privacy disclosures. Their action caused a trend of privacy initiatives by many companies using cyberspace. Marketplace expectations will dictate the level of privacy offered by business.

This study began by asserting that consumer attitudes would ultimately form privacy operational standards. The question is how can consumer concepts of privacy be utilized to guide electronic commerce, public policy, and develop financial education for under represented populations as a public affairs initiative. The study evolved to focus on the perceptions and attitudes of African Americans on financial privacy.

The project is an exploratory and descriptive study that assesses the privacy concerns of today's consumer, as well as determines the potential impact of consumer privacy concerns on technological innovation and public policy. In order to understand consumer privacy concerns, the study builds and extends current research on privacy in the financial services sector. The project expands the research conducted by Yankelovich Partners in 1994, the 1996 Equifax-Harris Consumer Privacy Survey, and the 1998 Privacy Concerns & Consumer Choice Survey by Louis Harris & Associates and Dr. Allan F. Westin.

The Yankelovich Study, the 1996 Equifax-Harris Consumer Privacy Survey, and the 1998 Privacy Concerns & Consumer Choice Survey were developed to assess the privacy concerns of consumers. Past studies were not designed to analyze or evaluate the specific impact of privacy on the African American consumer. The study expands this research to focus on the African American population. Using privacy as the foundational issue/motivation for developing perspectives on financial education, the study focuses on attitudes and perceptions of people of color in the financial mainstream of our economy.

PART ONE

EUROPEAN DATA PROTECTION

Globally, legislators and regulators continue to look closely at the issue of privacy and the collection and use of personal data. On October 24 1995, the European Union (EU) adopted the Data Protection Directive—a directive for transferring personal data to and from European countries. Specifically, when an EU country transfers such information to a non-EU country, the Data Protection Directive requires the country receiving the data to provide an "adequate level" of data protection. In addition, emphasis is on the use of "sensitive" personal information. However, what constitutes an "adequate level" of protection and "sensitive" personal information is not clear. The European definition and perception of adequate and sensitive are drastically different from other countries, particularly the United States. This requirement could substantially impact the ability of companies located outside the EU to receive data from a person or entity in an EU country.

The overall purpose of the Data Protection Directive is to protect the fundamental rights and freedoms of people, and in particular the right to privacy, with respect to the processing of personal data. The Data Protection Directive applies to all processing of personal data by any organization governed by EU law and, consequently, includes databases of both private and governmental organizations. (Directive 95/46/EC of the European Parliament and of the Council of the Protection of Individuals with Regard to the Processing of Personal Data and the Free Movement, October 24, 1995.)

Transfers of Personal Data to Third Countries

Article 25 of the Data Protection Directive impacts the transfer of personal data between Europe and the United States. Article 25.1 allows the transfer of personal data to a third country, i.e. the United States, for processing *only if* that country "ensures an adequate level of protection." Paragraph 6 of Article 25 of the Data Protection Directive describes the responsibility of determining which countries offer "adequate" protection. Under Article 25.2 of the Data Protection Directive, a country or a specific industry can be considered to ensure an adequate level of protection on a case by case basis. Each situation can be analyzed according to the nature of the data, the purpose and duration of the proposed processing operation(s), the country of origin and country of final destination, the rules of law, both general and sectoral, in force in the third country in question and the professional rules and security measures which are complied within that country. (Directive 95/46/EC of the European Parliament and of the Council of the Protection of Individuals with Regard to the Processing of Personal Data and the Free Movement, October 24, 1995.)

Because Article 25 is a very subjective and a political issue, a working party was set up by the EU Commission to manage the application of Article 25 and the determination of adequate privacy protection.

In the absence of adequate protection in the sense of Article 25.2, Article 26.2 of the Data Protection Directive enables *Member States* to allow data transfers to third countries without "adequate" data protection if the controller determines adequate safeguards with respect to the protection of the privacy. The Data Protection Directive adds that such safeguards may result from appropriate *contractual clauses*, which could result in the establishment of adequate safeguards on the basis of which a transfer could proceed. Member States must notify the EU Commission of any decision taken on the basis of Article 26.2. The EU Commission may take a position based on Article 26.4 of the Data Protection Directive.

The EU Commission is saying that the contractual solution is most effective where the parties to the contract are large operators already subject to public scrutiny and regulation. Large international corporations in highly regulated industries demonstrate both of these characteristics and more likely utilize contracts. (Page 23 of the EU Commission's Working Document on transfers of personal data to third countries). Article 26.4 of the Data Protection Directive gives power to the EU Commission, acting in accordance with the procedure in Article 31, to decide that certain standard contractual clauses offer the sufficient guarantees discussed in Article 26.2.

On April 22 1998, the EU Commission's Article 29 working group issued a report that endorses the "contractual solution" approach for compliance with the Data Protection Directive. The "working group" includes policy analysts assigned by the EU to review the Article 29 of the Data Protection Directive. The working group believes that the contractual approach deems private users of data as compliant with the directive if they incorporate adequate privacy guarantees into their contracts with consumers. Again, the definition of "adequate" is unclear. Many businesses have used the opinion of the working group to develop internal policies and procedures as a contractual approach to the directive. Larger companies will have an easier time of instituting a contractual approach. Smaller companies may have a more difficult time developing acceptable alternatives of compliance. Because the United States relies largely on a sector and self-regulatory approach, rather than a legislative approach to effective privacy protection, many U.S. organizations are uncertain about the impact of the "adequacy" standard on personal data transfers from the European Community to the United States. (Working Document: Preliminary views on the use of contractual provisions in the context of transfers of personal data to third countries, Working Party on the Protection of Individuals with regard to the Processing of Personal Data, April 22, 1998)

Publicly, the business industry has lobbied that applying the EU Data Protection Directive would be improper and severely detrimental to industry and its customers. Any disruption in the flow of data from the EU could, among other things, hinder a company's ability to cross-market to customers. A disruption of data exchange also could impede the ability of U.S. firms to acquire or form strategic alliances with EU firms. If the Data Protection Directive were enforced by the intent of European privacy protection, EU firms would be unable and reluctant to enter in any joint ventures with U.S. firms. To engage in any transactions with an entity in a non-compliant country would subject an EU firm to possible legal actions or sanctions.

Process of Data Stoppage (Source: Coalition of Service Industries)

The EU Data Commissioner will work with the company to solve the data problem by contract or a change in procedures. The EU Data Commissioner may also consult with Data Commissioners in other countries to see how they may have resolved a similar problem.

If adequacy in the third country cannot be established, the EU Data Commissioner will assess whether one of the exemptions in Article 26 apply, e.g. consent. If this is not the case, the Data Commissioner will see whether it can determine other safeguards, notably through contracts. During this process, the EU Data Commissioner may seek views of other Data Commissioners.

The objective of the EU Data Commissioner is to ensure that data are adequately protected when they are transferred to third countries. It is expected that it will seek assurances and explore solutions together with the company (in previous cases...there has always been very close co-operation between the Data Protection Authority and the company). The blocking of a transfer is normally a last resort after all other avenues have failed. The transfer will be allowed if adequacy is ensured. If the company does not take the necessary steps, the transfer will remain blocked. It is in the interest of the company not to delay this process.

1) If the data problem is not resolved, the EU Data Commissioner will stop the data flow and notify Member State officials.

2) The Members State officials will notify the Commission. The Commission will refer the data stoppage to the Article 31 Committee.

3) In 2 to 4 months, the Article 31 Committee will make a decision on the validity of the data stoppage. If the problem is not resolved, the transfer remains blocked and the Member State must inform the Commission. Subsequently, the Article 31 Committee will meet and the Commission will present a proposal of any measures to be taken (either to let the transfer go ahead or have it blocked for the whole of the EU). Member States will vote and the Commission will make the final decision. Member States can over-turn this decision by a Council decision (this is the so-called "comitology" procedure). There are no deadlines or firm rules of procedure other than those of Article 31.

4) If the Article 31 Committee decides it is a valid data stoppage, all Member States will stop data flows to the same company. If the Article 31 Committee decides it is not a valid data stoppage, the data stoppage will be lifted.

International Privacy Policies

Outside Europe the EU Data Protection Directive has a serious impact on international privacy concerns. The Russian State Duma–Russia's lower house of parliament–is considering a privacy statute similar to the one existing in Taiwan, which makes exporting data extremely difficult for businesses. Both laws apply specifically to computerized data processing and focuses on digital handling of data. It further requires that all entities (including business, governments, and individuals) obtain a license to process computerized data. The Federation of European Direct Marketing Associations unsuccessfully pushed to pass an alternate bill in the Duma, similar to the current United Kingdom law.

In Central and South America, legislators likewise are seeking privacy protections in response to the EU Data Protection Directive. The

Argentinean Chamber of Deputies, for example, is considering a data protection bill that expands citizens' Constitutional rights to review their personal data held by others. The bill is similar to the U.S. Freedom of Information Act. Meanwhile, in Chile, a comparable bill to that in Argentina is pending. This legislation, however, is more balanced and does not include business entities. A bill under consideration in Brazil establishes an enforcement body modeled on the EU Data Protection Directive that allows access, consent, and cross-border flow of data. Finally, in Mexico, an agency reporting to that country's Department of Commerce published a legally binding mandate requiring companies to obtain express consent before using or sharing personal financial data.

Legislative and regulatory activity has stepped up in the Pacific Rim, as well. In Australia, a nation historically concerned with protecting citizens' privacy, regulators issued the *National Principles*, which includes a principle about the identification of sensitive data. Regulators decided not to force the private sector to comply, instead allowing businesses to adopt the principles as a self-regulatory code. In Malaysia, a parliamentary drafting committee is developing a bill similar to the EU Data Protection Directive, while at the same time carefully studying the pending United Kingdom bill. The initial draft of this legislation parallels the latter statute, but is not yet available to the public. Japan is taking a self-regulatory approach to the issue of privacy and electronic commerce. In that country, business entities are required to develop and implement internal procedures to protect consumer data.

Finally, South Africa is drafting an "open democracy" bill (similar to the U.S. Freedom of Information Act) that would require written consent of consumers before their personal financial information can be used or shared.

In general, most countries are optimistic that the EU will take a flexible approach to implementing the Data Protection Directive. They will wait to see how the overall international community responds to and complies with the Data Protection Directive.

Following are responses from regions within Europe to the EU Data Protection Directive and privacy concerns.

Country	Current Law	EU Directive Compliance
Austria	Data Protection Act, 1978	Telcom, Genetic, Police sector laws passed. Draft implementation legislation circulated in March.
Belgium	Law on the Protection of Private Life Regarding the Processing of Personal Data, 1992	Council of State reviewed draft in January. Revised bill presented to Parliament in April.
Denmark	Public Registers Act, 1978 Private Registers Act, 1978	Bill submitted to Parliament in April.
Finland	Personal Data Files Act, 1987	Implementation bill expected soon.
France	Act on Data Processing, Data Files and Individual Liberties, 1978	Government drafting bill to implement EU Data Protection and EU Telcom Directive.
Germany	Federal Data Protection Act, 1977	Telcom, Information sector laws passed. Draft bill circulated in December 1997.
Greece Ireland	Data Protection Act, 1997 Data Protection Act, 1988	Follows directive closely. Consultation paper published. Government drafting implementation bill.
Italy	Act on the Protection of Individuals and Legal Persons Regarding the Processing of Personal Data, 1996	Current law partially implements the directive.

Luxembourg	Nominal Data Act, 1979	Bill presented to Parliament, withdrawn in September 1997. New bill being prepared.
Netherlands	Data Protection Act, 1988	Draft act submitted to Parliament in February.
Portugal	Protection of Personal Data Act, 1991	Constitution amended to include data protection in 1997. Bill submitted to Parliament in April.
Spain	Law on the Regulation of the Automated Processing of Personal Data, 1992	Draft law submitted to the Council of State in May.
Sweden	Data Protection Act, 1973	Bill submitted to Parliament in December 1997. New Personal Data Act published in May.
UK	Data Protection Act, 1984	Draft legislation introduced in January.
Country Gibraltar	Current Law	EU Directive Compliance Intends to legislate implementation with UK Data Protection Registrar to data protection functions.
Guernsey Hungary	Data Protection Law, 1986 Act on the Protection of Personal Data and Disclosure of Data of Public Interest, 1993	Current law to be revised. COE Convention 108 ratified 1997. Current law under review.

Iceland	Act Concerning the Registration and Handling of Personal Data, 1989	Current law under examination.
Poland	Data Protection Act, 1997	Closely follows directive.
Romania		Signed COE Convention 108, 1992. Government to update bill to comply with directive.
Slovakia	Law on Personal Data Protection in Information Systems, 1998	Current law closely follows directive.
Slovenia	Personal Data Protection Act, 1990	New proposal prepared to cover public and private sector.

Source: Maureen Feinroth, Privacy & American Business

Part Two

United States Privacy Policy

Although privacy is a concern in the United States, the concept of privacy is not specifically referenced in the United States Constitution. As a result, personal privacy is excluded as a constitutional right and the violation of an individual's privacy has no foundation for government action. Specifically, individuals do not have a Constitutional right to privacy. Therefore, defining privacy as it pertains to the individual consumer is not easily accomplished. (Bonavia, Morton). Privacy policy will have to focus on "privacy tolerance" as a concept of consumer acceptance versus a clear definition of what is privacy. In essence, the public will dictate what is acceptable by the current trend of tolerance. Today, consumers readily disclose social security numbers to complete a transaction or gain access to information. In the past, consumers were more apprehensive and considered such information very private. In the current environment, invasion of privacy has become more tolerable. The definition of privacy will fluctuate according to consumer acceptance. It is easier to describe privacy than to give a definition. Common practices in today's marketplace have set the standard of privacy tolerance. Consumers readily give personal information in the process of completing many transactions. Unconsciously, the consumer reveals crucial information with the idea that the information given is necessary to complete the transaction. For example, it is not necessary or required to give your name, address, or phone number for non-warranty cash and carry merchandise. However, most consumers will easily disclose such information when requested.

This varies drastically from the European perspective and practice of privacy as a constitutional right.

In the United States, the Clinton Administration is focusing more on privacy issues from the U.S. perspective and, to some extent, on the Data Protection Directive. With the heightened sensitivity to electronic commerce and information technology, the Clinton Administration has increased pressure to regulate privacy—especially relating to the Internet. In response, many government agencies are conducting privacy initiatives. As these agencies analyze privacy in the United States, officials anticipate that technology will offer security solutions to many privacy concerns particularly in an evolving information age. If privacy concerns are not addressed by industry through self-regulation and technology, the government under the forces of development will itself be forced to institute legislative and regulatory protection of consumer privacy.

Electronic Bill of Rights

Vice President Gore has taken an increasingly visible role in privacy issues. On May 14, 1998, Vice President Gore called for establishment of an "Electronic Bill of Rights" to protect the general privacy of Americans in the electronic age. Gore's plan calls for reliance on private sector leader-ship where possible, backed up by federal government action, including legislation, when necessary. This set the stage for privacy protection in the future. It is clear that this will be a campaign issue for the 2000 presidential election. Ironically, Vice President Gore created a nexus with privacy being an American value and a right, similar to the European perspective of data protection. Privacy is not a right under the United States Constitution and the American value of privacy is far less restrictive than the European perspective.

The Vice President focused on key elements of privacy protection: notice, consent, awareness, and verification. He further advocated for the business industry to "do their part to protect individual privacy." To add incentive, the Vice President announced new action in four key areas:

- protecting sensitive personal information
- taking new executive action
- calling for tough new legislation to protect personal information such as medical and financial records
- ensuring that existing privacy laws are strong enough to protect privacy as technology grows and changes

Encouraging the "voluntary private sector action to protect privacy" balances a liberal agenda with a pro–business direction. He challenges the private sector to continue to take effective voluntary steps to protect privacy on-line while suggesting that legislation was possible.

Vice President Gore also indicated that the Administration would work with Congress to pass legislation that would make it a federal crime to obtain confidential customer information from a bank by fraudulent means. While the 105th Congress considered such legislation, it was not enacted. The current political status remains uncertain.

The Vice President will continue to take an active role in new privacy legislation. Legislation to protect personal information such as medical and financial records is inevitable. The foundation has been set by the Administration directives to Treasury and the banking regulators to strengthen the enforcement of the Fair Credit Reporting Act with respect to the sharing of information between banks and their affiliates and "opt-out" notices for consumers. The Administration will also ask that Congress give bank regulators the authority to examine financial institutions for compliance with the Fair Credit Reporting Act. In addition, the Administration will work with the Federal Trade Commission to encourage companies that build dossiers about individuals by aggregating information from a variety of database sources to implement effective self-regulatory mechanisms. If industry attempts at self-regulation are not successful, the Administration will consider other means to ensure adequate privacy protection. (July 31, 1998, The White House, Office of the Vice President)

Federal Trade Commission

The Federal Trade Commission (FTC) has been extremely active in privacy issues in recent years. The increased attention is in anticipation and preparation of consumer demand. During 1996 and 1997, the FTC held a series of public workshops on privacy issues. The workshops focused on a number of topics, including the possible use of the FTC's existing authority under the Federal Trade Commission Act to bring enforcement actions against entities whose privacy practices could be characterized as "unfair or deceptive." The FTC also conducted a highly publicized study of so-called "look-up services," that is, of computerized data bases that contain sensitive consumer identifying information. In December 1997, the FTC released a report on the study, entitled *Individual Reference Services: A Report to Congress* (Look-Up Services Report). Importantly, in the Look-Up Services Report, the FTC recognized that, by providing convenient access to information about individuals, look-up services provide many benefits to users of these services and to society at large. Nonetheless, the FTC points out that the availability of information through look-up services poses various risks, such as a potential threat to individual privacy and harm from unlawful uses of personal identifying information, including identity theft and credit card fraud. (Individual Reference Services: A Report to Congress, Federal Trade Commission, December, 1997)

On July 21, 1998, the FTC testified on Internet privacy issues before the Subcommittee on Telecommunications, Trade and Consumer Protection of the House Committee on Commerce. At the hearing, FTC Chairman Pitofsky delivered testimony on behalf of the FTC Commissioners proposing an agenda for administrative action. Pitofsky told the Subcommittee that, while the FTC remains hopeful that private industry self-regulation will achieve adequate online privacy protections for consumers, current industry self-regulatory initiatives are inadequate. Pitofsky said "the Commission believes that, unless industry can demonstrate that it has developed and implemented broad-based and effective self-regulatory programs by the end of this year, additional governmental authority in this area would be appropriate and necessary." (Prepared Statement of the Federal Trade Commission on Consumer Privacy on the World Wide Web, Subcommittee on Telecommunications, Trade, and Consumer Protection, July 21,1998, Chairman Robert Pitofsky)

In the testimony, Pitofsky also described proposed legislation, which the FTC believes, would, if enacted, adequately protect consumer privacy online. It will also serve as a broad action front for the FTC to regulate consumer privacy and give consumers a tactical structure to determine privacy online. Under the proposed legislation, all commercial Web sites that collect personal identifying information from or about consumers online would be required to comply with four basic information practices. First, Web sites would be required to provide consumers notice of their information practices, including what information they collect and how they use it. Second, Web sites must provide consumers with a choice of how their information is used beyond the purpose for which the information was provided. Third, Web sites would be required to offer consumers reasonable access to their information and an opportunity to correct inaccuracies. Finally, Web sites must take reasonable steps to protect the security and integrity of personal information. (Prepared Statement of the Federal Trade Commission on Consumer Privacy on the World Wide Web, Subcommittee on Telecommunications, Trade, and Consumer Protection, July 21,1998, Chairman Robert Pitofsky)

The proposed legislation includes a "safe harbor" to encourage industry self-regulatory initiatives. Under the proposed legislation, a Web site's compliance with government-certified guidelines developed by private industry would provide a safe harbor from enforcement actions under this new legislation. The safe harbor would not, however, protect an entity from failure to comply with other statutes, including the Federal Trade Commission Act's prohibition on "unfair and deceptive" practices.

Pitofsky also recommended that Congress provide one federal agency with rule-making authority under the proposed legislation.

The Federal Trade Commission released a report titled *Privacy Online: A Report to Congress June 1998*. The report was the result of the commission's three-year privacy initiative to analyze the effectiveness of self-regulation as a means of protecting consumer data on the World Wide Web. The Federal Trade Commission surveyed 1,402 Web sites, taking 674 sites as a sample. The survey found that a significant number of sites are collecting personally identifiable information (92% of the sites surveyed, although the type of sites surveyed may have artificially increased that percentage). Of these sites almost all (98%) collected email address and 68% collected a name. Two-thirds of the sites that collected a name and/or email address were collecting one or more types of information and almost half were collecting three or more types of information. Despite the large number of sites collecting information, only 14% had some kind of disclosure of what they were doing with personal data.

The report divided surveyed the Web sites into six categories: (a) "comprehensive," general-interest sites; (b) health-related sites; (c) retail sites; (d) financial sites; (e) child-oriented sites; and (f) "most popular" sites. These figures show a clear lack of industry attention to even the most basic of fair information practices. The privacy policy gap between the most popular sites and the Internet as a whole is particularly interesting, suggesting that the attention on the issue over the past three years has been mostly heard by a select number of larger businesses online. (CDT Analysis of the Federal Trade Commission Report on Online, Center for Democracy and Technology, www.cdt.org.)

Overall, the report revealed that only a small percentage of the 1,400 Web sites surveyed provide any notice of their data collection practices, and only 2% provide a comprehensive privacy policy. The Federal Trade Commission concludes that Web sites "demonstrate the real need for implementing basic fair information practices." These practices are necessary to protect consumer privacy interests. The Federal Trade Commission has identified a set of core principles for information collection, use, and dissemination. "The core principles require that consumers be given notice of an entity's information practices; that consumers be given choice with respect to the use and dissemination of information collected and stored by an entity; and that consumers be given access to information about them collected and stored by an entity; and that the data collector take appropriate steps to ensure the security and integrity of any data collected. Moreover, it is widely recognized that fair information practice codes or guidelines should contain enforcement mechanisms to ensure compliance with these core principles."(Privacy Online: A Report to Congress, Federal Trade Commission, June 1998.)

These "fair information practice principles" were first developed by the United States Department of Health, Education, and Welfare's 1973 report entitled "Records, Computers and the Rights of Citizens." The report is the foundation of the Privacy Act of 1974, which addresses government management of personal information. The Federal Trade Commission has used these principles as a framework for online privacy and has directed online entities to adopt them in online activities. Specifically in the areas of: Notice/Awareness, Choice/Consent, Access/Participation and Enforcement/Redress.

Despite the attention by the United States government, the Federal Trade Commission found that self-regulation and increased consumer concern about privacy on the Internet has not generated effective action or response by the business community while business has increased efforts to collect personal information via the Internet. The actual results of the report detect the surface issue overlaying the collecting of personal data online. The natural next step concerns whether personal data was used according to stated privacy policies and whether the businesses provide adequate protection. This survey examined whether Web sites were taking the first step of posting a policy but did not inquire further. The Federal Trade Commission recommended that Congress develop legislation to require sites that collect: (1) offline contact information, (2) publicly posted information, or (3) information to be disclosed to third-parties from children under 13 obtain prior parental consent. (CDT Analysis of the Federal Trade Commission Report on Online, Center for Democracy and Technology, www.cdt.org.)

It is unclear how the Federal Trade Commission will proceed. However, the Federal Trade Commission has strategically positioned enforcement of online privacy. Pressure by advocacy groups has forced the development of consequences for those that do not comply with the suggested privacy principles. The enforcement will not terminate the collection of personal data but will force business to disclose the use of information. The effectiveness of disclosure has long been debated as a compromise solution. Currently, disclosure is the only basis for enforcement and its legal basis is still under developed.

In August of 1998, the Federal Trade Commission began enforcement action of privacy violations on GeoCities, a large, online "community builder", in which the Federal Trade Commission alleged that the company had improperly collected and used information obtained from individuals through its Web site. This is the first time that the Federal Trade Commission has brought charges against a company arising from a failure to protect consumers' privacy on the Internet. (Intellectual Property and Technology Law Letter, Morgan, Lewis, & Bockius, volume 6, number 7, September 1998.)

At the time of the investigation by the Federal Trade Commission, GeoCities' online application form requested personal identifying information from new members and indicated that certain sensitive "optional information" would not be released to anyone without a member's permission. The Federal Trade Commission found that GeoCities did disclose members' personal data to third parties who used it to solicit sales for goods and services that members did not request. (Intellectual Property and Technology Law Letter, Morgan, Lewis, & Bockius, volume 6, number 7, September 1998.)

The Federal Trade Commission has indicated that this case signifies a warning to all online marketers that statements about their information collection practices must be accurate and complete. The Commission has emphasized that it will continue monitoring Web sites and will bring additional enforcement actions, as appropriate. Because of no legal precedence the Federal Trade Commission did not require GeoCities to pay monetary damages. Companies found to violate consumers' online privacy may be found liable for damages. This situation has increased the issue of privacy for businesses and created an unprecedented sensitivity to the recommended privacy principles. Without Congressional legislation, overall impact will be limited. Congress has not given the Federal Trade Commission a mandate to specifically regulate privacy protection. (Intellectual Property and Technology Law Letter, Morgan, Lewis, & Bockius, volume 6, number 7, September 1998.)

United States Department of Commerce

The United States Department of Commerce held a two-day summit in June 1998 to explore issues relating to privacy for electronic commerce. The summit explored the privacy issue with the industry, academics, public interest groups, and the international community. The Commerce Department, along with the Office of Management and Budget were asked to report to the President on industry efforts to establish self-regulatory regimes to ensure privacy online and to develop technological solutions to protect privacy. The President also directed the Commerce Department and the Office of Management and Budget to ensure that means are developed to protect children's privacy online. The Commerce Department requested comments on various aspects of Internet Privacy including the effectiveness of self-regulation for privacy. Specifically, the Commerce Department wanted comments on the staff discussion paper "Elements of Effective Self Regulation for Protection of Privacy." (National Telecommunications and Information Administration, United States Department of Commerce, privacy @ntia.doc.gov)

The discussion paper further refines four core principles and sets out nine specific characteristics of effective self-regulation for privacy: awareness, choice, data security, data integrity, consumer access, accountability, consumer recourse, verification and consequences. The paper notes that individual industry sectors will need to develop their own methods of providing the necessary requirements of self-regulation. The Department of Commerce wanted industry to comment specifically on the elements set out in the draft discussion paper that deal with enforcement (verification, recourse, and consequences) and suggest ways in which companies and industry sectors might implement these. This aspect to privacy is similar to the European Directive approach. (Elements of Effective Self-Regulation for Protection of Privacy, A Staff Discussion Draft, United States Department of Commerce)

The President has directed the Department of Commerce and the Office of Management and Budget to work with the private sector to develop and implement effective, consumer-friendly, self-regulatory privacy regimes. The Clinton Administration supports private sector efforts to implement effective self-regulatory privacy regimes for the Internet. These include mechanisms for facilitating consumer awareness of privacy principles and the exercise of choice about whether and under what circumstances to disclose personal information online, evaluating private sector adoption of and adherence to fair information practices, and dispute resolution. The Clinton Administration also anticipates that technology tools will empower consumers to exercise choices about their privacy. In the section on consequences, the draft discussion paper states that "sanctions should be stiff enough to be meaningful and swift enough to assure consumers that their concerns are addressed in a timely fashion." Existing laws and regulations are not capable of providing harsh or stiff sanctions and the United States legal process prevents immediate response from authorities to be meaningful in respect to public awareness. This presents the underlying purpose and outcome of the discussion draft. Government authorities are relying on business to provide industry regulations to protect consumers. (Elements of Effective Self-Regulation for Protection of Privacy, NTIA, Federal Register, June 5, 1998)

The threat of European sanctions against the United States has forced the U.S. Department of Commerce, on behalf of the U.S. Government, to enter into negotiations with and Directorate General XV of the European Commission on Privacy. In a November 4, 1998 letter, the Department of Commerce claims to have discovered that, "despite our differences in approach, there is a great deal of overlap between U.S. and EU views on privacy." This is a significant development given the philosophical differences on privacy of the United States and Europeans.

The uncertainty of the Data Protection Directive's effect on transborder data transfers from Europe to the United States have forced the European Commission and the Department of Commerce to discuss the creation of a safe harbor for U.S. companies that choose "voluntarily" to adhere to certain privacy principles. Organizations within the safe harbor would have a presumption of adequacy and data transfers from Europe would continue. Companies could come within the safe harbor by self-certifying that they adhere to certain privacy principles. Companies that decide not to utilize the safe harbor could have data transfers interrupted.

These safe harbors allow the Clinton Administration to compromise with the European Commission while maintaining U.S. views on privacy. The safe harbor principles are based on the Elements for Effective Privacy Protection discussion paper, the 1980 Organization for Economic Cooperation and Development (OECD) Privacy Guidelines, private sector self-regulation, online privacy programs, and discussions with industry and the European Commission. The safe harbor principles are not intended to govern or affect U.S. privacy regimes, which are being addressed by other government and private sector efforts. Interestingly, the European Commission has not approved the safe harbor concept.

(Undersecretary David L. Aaron, United States Department of Commerce, November 4, 1998)

Analysis of Proposed Safe Harbor Privacy Principles

(Source: Coalition of Service Industries, November, 1998)

The proposed Safe Harbor Principles apply to information that the organization obtains directly from the individual or from private third parties. This does not include data from public (government) records, or information in the public domain, such as information that is published or broadcast. The Draft International Safe Harbor Privacy Principles are as follows:

1. **NOTICE:** An organization must inform individuals about what types of personal information it collects about them, how it collects that information, the purposes for which it collects such information, the types of organizations to which it discloses the information, and the choices and means the organization offers individuals for limiting its use and disclosure. This notice must be provided in clear and conspicuous language that is readily understood and made available when individuals are first asked to provide personal information to the organization.

2. **CHOICE:** An organization must give individuals the opportunity to choose (opt-out choice) whether and how personal information they provide is used (where such use is unrelated to the use(s) for which they originally disclosed it). They must be provided with clear and conspicuous, readily available, and affordable mechanisms to exercise this option. For certain kinds of sensitive information, such as medical information, they must be given affirmative or explicit (opt-in) choice.

3. **ONWARD TRANSFER:** Individuals must be given the opportunity to choose whether and the manner in which a third party uses the personal information they provide (when such use is unrelated to the use(s) for which the individual originally disclosed it). When transferring personal information to third parties, an organization must require that third parties provide at least the same level of privacy protection as originally chosen by the individual. For certain kinds of

sensitive information, such as medical information, individuals must be given opt-in choice.

4. **SECURITY:** Organizations creating, maintaining, using or disseminating records of personal information must take reasonable measures to assure its reliability for its intended use and must take reasonable precautions to protect it from loss, misuse, unauthorized access or disclosure, alteration, or destruction.

5. **DATA INTEGRITY:** An organization must keep personal data relevant for the purposes for which it has been gathered only, consistent with the principles of notice and choice. To the extent necessary for those purposes, the data should be accurate, complete, and current.

6. **ACCESS:** Individuals must have reasonable access to information about them derived from non public records that an organization holds and be able to correct or amend that information where it is inaccurate. Reasonableness of access depends on the nature and sensitivity of the information collected and its intended uses. For instance, access must be provided to an individual where the information in question is sensitive or used for substantive decision-making purposes that affect that individual.

7. **ENFORCEMENT:** Effective privacy protection must include mechanisms for assuring compliance with the principles, recourse for individuals, and consequences for the organization when the principles are not followed. At a minimum, such mechanisms must include (a) readily available and affordable independent recourse mechanisms by which individuals' complaints and disputes can be resolved; (b) systems for verifying that the attestations and assertions businesses make about their privacy practices are true and privacy practices have been implemented as presented; and (c) obligations to remedy problems arising out of and consequences for organizations announcing adoption of these principles and failing to comply with the principles. Sanctions must be sufficient to ensure compliance by organizations and must provide individuals the means for enforcement.

Note: Organizations may satisfy the requirements set forth in Principle 7: (a) through compliance with private sector developed privacy programs that include effective enforcement mechanisms of the type described in Principle 7; or (b) through compliance with legal or regulatory supervisory authorities; or (c) by committing to cooperate with data protection authorities located in the European Community.

Source: United States Department of Commerce, November 4, 1998

Because the Principles apply only to European data, the emphasis on international is misleading and should not be construed as internationally accepted. An appropriate title would be "European Union Safe Harbor Privacy Principles." Although the title is more reflective of the content, it would decrease the impact of the Data Protection Directive by suggesting potential loopholes to the Directive. Global acceptance of the safe harbor would be more difficult than enforcing the Data Protection Directive. The International Safe Harbor Principles presumes acceptance and acknowledgment of the Data Protection Directive.

The term "sensitive information" is used several times in the Principles document. It has a precise meaning for Europeans that may be different than the United States generally accepted meaning of sensitive. In Europe, sensitive information is information that reveals a person's racial or ethnic origin, political, religious, or philosophical views, labor union activity, or information about a person's health or sexuality. In the United States, sensitive generally applies to information about personal health or finances.

The term "readily understood" is unclear and subject to multiple definitions. The term attempts to define "interpretation" as a result. Emphasis has been established earlier in the sentence by the requirement that notice must be provided in "clear language." Clear language is far more recognizable and definable than "readily understood."

The requirement for *third party privacy protection* specifies that the organization to which information is transferred provide the same level of privacy as originally chosen by the individual. The requirement contradicts current U.S. law allowing affiliate sharing. The Fair Credit Reporting

Act allows affiliate sharing of customer information with other subsidiaries of the same corporation.

By requiring *data to be current*, implies a requirement to update old, even archived, records. In addition, the requirement that *an organization may keep data relevant only for the purposes for which it has been gathered*, may conflict with regulatory requirements that some data be maintained that is not relevant only for the purposes for which acquired. The banking industry is required to collect individual Social Security Numbers or face fines and sanctions.

In applying the *access principle*, an organization would provide access to an individual's transaction record and the factual bases for business decisions that significantly affect the individual. This also could require a creditor to reveal information concerning credit scoring for borrowers. This information on modeling techniques could be subject to intellectual property protection.

The *enforcement* requirement opens a wide range of possibilities for individuals in pursuit of enforcement. This has always been highly contentious for the business industry and a foundational difference between European privacy law and existing U.S. attitude on privacy protection. The U.S. government advocates a self-regulatory approach with the Federal Trade Commission, financial services regulatory authority, and state attorney generals serving as a soft influence. Currently, individuals have rights conferred by legal action in U.S. courts based on breach of contract laws.

While a committee representing the fifteen European Union member states voted to reject the Proposed Safe Harbor Privacy Principles on November 19, 1998, U.S. officials have publicly stated that they are optimistic that the proposal can be "refined" to address European concerns. In particular, it is reported that differences remain over whether individuals can have access to personal information held by companies—an idea strongly opposed by U.S. industry. Differences also reportedly exist over the European's desire to establish a monitoring entity that would assure

European Commission authorities that U.S. companies were adhering to the requirements of the Proposed Safe Harbor Privacy Principles. European and U.S. negotiators recently announced that they would miss their self-imposed deadline of yearend for resolving these differences.

PART THREE

FINANCIAL SECTOR PRIVACY

The focus of this section is to review specific privacy activity with the financial sector. The financial sector has an obligation to protect consumer privacy by law and obligation. Because the United States monetary system would not function without consumer confidence, privacy has become a safety and soundness issue.

Office of the Comptroller of the Currency

The Office of the Comptroller of the Currency (OCC) was established in 1863 as a bureau of the Department of the Treasury. It is responsible for regulating and supervising the national banking system. The OCC also supervises and regulates the federally licensed branches and agencies of foreign banks doing business in the United States. Though the mission of the agency has remained constant over the years, changes in the external environment have required a new strategy to manage the evolution of the banking industry. Currently, accelerating advances in technology are changing the fundamental nature of how information is created, processed and delivered. (Office of the Comptroller of the Currency Web site, November, 1998)

The OCC has taken probably the most visible role of the federal banking agencies in addressing privacy issues. Since April 1998, the OCC has waged a high-profile campaign to urge the banking industry to undertake more aggressive leadership in consumer privacy issues. The acting Comptroller of the Currency, Ms. Julie Williams has repeatedly cautioned that if banking industry self-regulatory initiatives are not strengthened, the stage will be set for a more active government role which could result in restrictions on the ability of banks to collect and use information. In particular, she remains concerned that the enforcement provisions of many self-regulatory initiatives are too weak.

In May 1998, as part of her privacy campaign, the OCC established the OCC Privacy Working Group to evaluate the performance of, and develop guidance for, national banks in addressing various privacy issues. The Privacy Working Group is comprised of senior staff from a number of key OCC divisions.

In June 1998, the Privacy Working Group was directed to develop guidance for national banks to address a number of consumer privacy issues, including Web site disclosures of bank privacy policies, sharing of customer information, information security and identity theft. More specifically, the Privacy Working Group was assigned to develop model disclosures that can be used by national banks to inform consumers about an institution's information sharing practices and the rights customers have under the Fair Credit Reporting Act to opt-out of affiliate information sharing. In addition, the Privacy Working Group was to develop "effective practices" for Internet disclosure of banks' privacy policies to be displayed in a clear and conspicuous manner. The overall objective was to develop recommendations for national banks regarding adequate internal controls to assure that confidential customer information is safeguarded from improper disclosure and from identity theft.

The objectives of the Privacy Working Group have evoked strong criticism from some key lawmakers. In response to affiliate sharing directives to the Privacy Working Group, three prominent members of the House Banking Committee urged the OCC to "move slowly in this area" and requested that the OCC consult with them before it takes any action on affiliate sharing. They wanted to "ensure that the congressional intent behind these reforms is honored." Noting that they were the lead sponsors of the Fair Credit Reporting Act affiliate sharing amendments, the

Congressmen said their intent was to permit financial institutions to fully share information among their affiliates, with only minimal limitations and procedural requirements. "In particular," the Congressmen wrote, "we intended to ensure that companies not be disadvantaged by being in a holding company structure and that information sharing among bank affiliates should be done in a manner comparable to information sharing within a bank itself or within any other single company." In addition, the Congressmen noted that, when considering amendments to the Fair Credit Reporting Act, the House Banking Committee specifically rejected other efforts to place further burdens on information sharing. Thus, "it would be problematic if any regulatory actions would upset the delicate balance" achieved in the Fair Credit Reporting Act's affiliate sharing provisions. (McCollum, Bereuter, and Baker Letter to Acting Comptroller Williams, October 26, 1998.)

On August 3, 1998, the OCC issued a bulletin on the Fair Credit Reporting Act and the sharing of consumer information from consumer reports and affiliated companies. The bulletin attempted to summarize the rights and responsibilities of national banks under the Fair Credit Reporting Act. Contrary to the description, the bulletin was an exertion of power by the OCC to further examine banks for compliance with the Fair Credit Reporting Act.

As of September 30, 1997 the Economic Growth and Regulatory Paperwork Reduction Act of 1996 (EGRPRA) substantially amended the Fair Credit Reporting Act. While providing new opportunities for banks to use and share customer information with affiliated companies, the amended statues significantly limited the authority of federal financial institution supervisory agencies to examine banks for compliance with the Fair Credit Reporting Act. (Sources: Economic Growth and Regulatory Paperwork Reduction Act of 1996, Fair Credit Reporting Act of 1970)

According to EGRPRA, agencies can not exam a bank for compliance with the Fair Credit Reporting Act unless the agency has received a complaint that the bank is in violation of the law. However, the Fair Credit

Reporting Act does not specify what constitutes a compliant, what circumstances constitute and examination of a complaint, or the scope of the examination. (Office of the Comptroller of the Currency Bulletin 98-33, August 3, 1998)

The OCC bulletin interpreted the Fair Credit Reporting Act within the jurisdiction of the agency. The OCC will conduct an examination to investigate all complaints. During the course of the investigation, the OCC will consider any information that they deem pertinent for determining validity. In addition, the investigation will not be limited to a specific transaction or set of transactions. If the OCC determines a violation of the Fair Credit Reporting Act has occurred, the OCC will conduct a full examination. Lastly, the OCC will conduct an examination if the agency "otherwise has knowledge." (Office of the Comptroller of the Currency Bulletin 98-33, August 3, 1998)

This last provision is the most drastic interpretation. The Fair Credit Reporting Act provides no specific guidance on what constitutes "otherwise has knowledge." However, the OCC believes that any specific information about violations of the Fair Credit Reporting Act may trigger an investigation. This effectively informs the banking industry that the Clinton Administration is positioning the banking industry as a test case to apply stricter privacy laws and regulation. Unlike the voluntary aspect of International Safe Harbor Privacy Principles, the OCC can mandate banks to protect consumer privacy. These are two distinctly different tactics by the Department of Commerce and the OCC. (Office of the Comptroller of the Currency Bulletin 98-33, August 3, 1998)

Office of Thrift Supervision

The Financial Institutions Reform, Recovery, and Enforcement Act of 1989 established the Office of Thrift Supervision (OTS) to examine and supervise savings and loan associations and federal savings banks. The OTS replaces the Federal Home Loan Bank Board as primary regulator of state chartered and federally chartered savings institutions. The agency is a bureau within the United States Treasury Department. The structure of the OTS parallels the Office of the Comptroller of the Currency. (Office of Thrift Supervision Web site, November 1998)

The OTS recently issued guidance on privacy issues. More specifically, on November 3, 1998, the OTS released a "Policy Statement on Privacy and Accuracy of Personal Customer Information" (Policy Statement) which, according to the OTS, reflects some "best practices" that may help thrifts adequately protect personal information. However, the Policy Statement takes a very broad approach, much of which goes far beyond any existing federal law or regulation, creating significant legal and regulatory compliance uncertainty for savings associations. (Policy Statement on Privacy and Accuracy of Personal Customer Information, Office of Thrift Supervision, November 3, 1998)

For instance, the Policy Statement recommends that thrifts provide an extensive disclosure to customers about how their information will be used. More specifically, it recommends that such a notice explain to the customer: (1) *all* intended uses of the personal information collected; (2) whether the thrift intends to sell or give the personal information to an affiliated or unaffiliated party; (3) what happens if the customer declines to provide the required information; (4) a general description of the methods used to assure the confidentiality and accuracy of information; and (5) a phone number, email address, or other point of contact that the customer can use to review and correct personal information, and to notify the institution about possible unauthorized access to, or use of, an account. This creates a number of issues for savings associations. With respect to disclosure of "all intended uses" of the personal information collected, it is not clear at what level of detail "uses" must be disclosed. In addition, what if a subsequent use was not disclosed? Or, if uses subsequently change, is the savings association obligated to make new disclosures to consumers? The Policy Statement provides no answers to these or similar questions. (Policy Statement on

Privacy and Accuracy of Personal Customer Information, Office of Thrift Supervision, November 3, 1998)

The Policy Statement states that these disclosures should be provided *before* any information is collected from the customer. This appears exhaustive and unworkable in that it would require that extensive disclosures be made to consumers before obtaining even impersonal information, like identification information. Marketing efforts also would be severely hampered, because a consumer inquiry or request for information about a product would first require the savings association to make the lengthy disclosures. (Policy Statement on Privacy and Accuracy of Personal Customer Information, Office of Thrift Supervision, November 3, 1998)

In addition, while noting that the Fair Credit Reporting Act requires that customers be provided the opportunity to opt-out of sharing with affiliated entities, the Policy Statement recommends that savings associations offer customers the choice to opt-out of having this information shared with unaffiliated third parties as well. Going even further, the Policy Statement implies that an *opt-in* may be required for certain sharing. It states that, "if the customer has chosen to limit the sharing of personal information, a savings association may not exchange or sell information about the customer to third parties unless it receives the *customer's request or permission* to release the information." The Policy Statement also recommends new obligations for savings associations that are similar to the Fair Credit Reporting Act obligations for credit bureaus by requiring that customers be able to review information the savings association has about them and correct inaccurate or outdated information. It also creates potential privacy and security issues by suggesting that savings associations provide such access by email. (Policy Statement on Privacy and Accuracy of Personal Customer Information, Office of Thrift Supervision, November 3, 1998)

Federal Deposit Insurance Corporation

The Federal Deposit Insurance Corporation (FDIC) manages the Bank Insurance Fund and the Savings Association Insurance Fund, which insures deposits in commercial banks and deposits in savings and loan associations, respectively. As a regulator, the FDIC can serve as the conservator or receiver for troubled banks. (Federal Deposit Insurance Corporation Web site, November 1998

In order to provide guidance for financial institutions in addressing consumer privacy issues, FDIC released a financial institution letter. This 1998 letter was entitled "Online Privacy of Consumer Personal Information" (Privacy Letter). In the Privacy Letter, the FDIC states that, "as a follow up to the Federal Trade Commission's survey of Web site privacy practices, the FDIC conducted an informal survey of financial institution Web sites." The Privacy Letter reports that the FDIC's findings were "comparable to" the Federal Trade Commission's. Specifically, the FDIC found that, while many sites conduct information collection, privacy statements are frequently altogether absent from bank Web sites. (Online Privacy of Consumer Personal Information, Federal Deposit Insurance Corporation, August 17, 1998)

The Privacy Letter urges each institution to establish and follow a "responsible" privacy policy, and suggests that each such privacy policy should include the "fair information practice principles" articulated by the Federal Trade Commission in its June 1998 report to Congress on online privacy issues. These principles are: (1) notice to the consumer; (2) consumer choice about the collection and use of their personal information; (3) adequate security and accuracy of collected information; and (4) consumer access to their collected information and ability to correct errors. The Privacy Letter states that the first principle, providing notice to the consumer, "may be the most important action taken by a financial institution." According to the FDIC, notice should include information about the other four principles, which will permit consumers to make an informed choice about the level of protection they want *before* providing personal information. Notice also should include the identity of the information collector; how the information is collected; why the information is collected; how the information will be used (particularly for secondary purposes), and how a consumer may limit the disclosure of information. While this notice guidance is more limited than that in the OTS Policy Statement, it raises many of the same issues for financial institutions—particularly related to the adequacy and timing of disclosure. The Privacy Letter concludes by stating that the FDIC supports industry self-regulation that is specific, meaningful and effective. (Online Privacy of Consumer Personal Information, Federal Deposit Insurance Corporation, August 17, 1998)

Financial Services Industry

According to the financial industry, U.S. financial institutions are more than adequately protecting customer confidentiality. The industry contends that the United States should not respond to the EU Data Protection Directive by imposing new requirements on U.S. financial institutions. According to the report, the United States already has comprehensive privacy laws and regulations. (Financial Privacy In America, A Review of Consumer Financial Services Issues, June, 1998)

Since the threat of the European Data Protection Directive, the financial services industry has advocated for industry-specific solutions. The industry believes that "rigid privacy standards of general application would stifle the flow of information, impose unnecessary costs and impede creative business innovations designed to benefit customers." (Financial Privacy In America, A Review of Consumer Financial Services Issues, June 1998). The foundation of the argument resides in the existing legal and regulatory environment for the financial industry. Ironically, the existing laws and regulation are a direct effect of the savings and loans crisis of the 1980's. Because of the recent history of

Congress targeting the industry as a test case for many "popular" concerns, the financial services sector is valid in its concern of increased legislative and regulatory activity on privacy.

Financial institutions are chartered, licensed and regulated by federal and state agencies. The mandate of these agencies is focussed on the safety and soundness of the institutions. Privacy has only been implied as a safety and soundness issue. The concern for specific privacy regulation has been promoted by the media and general public concern.

The financial services industry has long used personal information as a method to provide security to the consumer and the financial institution from fraud, credit risk/losses and bankruptcy losses. (Financial Privacy In America, A Review of Consumer Financial Services Issues, June 1998) Although security remains a valid issue for financial services, market competition has forced the industry to gather more intelligence about both potential and existing customers. Information gathered for security purposes became a valuable resource for marketing purposes. The industry has positioned the collection of information as a benefit to the consumer.

While financial Institutions increase their ability to capture and manage data, personal information has been marketed as a "preference" benefit to consumers. According to the industry, personal information allows businesses to offer products and services more closely aligned with consumers' needs and desires. The argument is based on consumer willingness to disclose personal information as an increase in awareness of these benefits. A study on attitudes on telemarketing and mail solicitation would be beneficial in evaluating the validity of the argument. (Financial Privacy In America, A Review of Consumer Financial Services Issues, June, 1998)

The balance between the free flow of information and protecting consumer privacy within the financial sector is rooted in existing law. In 1970, Congress enacted the original Fair Credit Reporting Act to govern the use of credit information. Because credit is such a basic part of American life, errors in or the misuse of credit information can cause great harm, e.g.—the mistaken denial of a mortgage to buy a house or the loss of an employment opportunity. In 1974, Congress enacted the Privacy Act to focus on protecting individuals when the government collects and uses personal information or shares data with contractors and other private parties. (Financial Privacy In America, A Review of Consumer Financial Services Issues, June, 1998)

In 1976, Congress revisited the issue of federal privacy legislation after the U.S. Supreme Court held that there was no legitimate "expectation of privacy" with regard to the contents of checks and deposit slips. The Fourth Amendment does not protect bank records. (*United States v. Miller,* 425 U.S. 435 (1976) Congress also established the United States Privacy Protection Study Commission to review issues relating to personal privacy. The Commission identified a series of basic privacy principles in its 1977 report to Congress and raised the possibility of comprehensive federal privacy legislation. Congress did not expand comprehensive legal coverage to private information systems.

Government has addressed financial privacy as a process within other activities. The protection of consumer privacy will not be directly addressed in the financial industry until Americans separate privacy from security and awareness is increased. Regulators have begun to respond to European pressure and the outcome will be stronger interpretation of existing laws. However, enforcement will be limited to existing laws that address financial privacy. Financial institutions are more susceptible to increased legislation due to the prevalence of strict guidelines. Although these guidelines are promulgated on safety and soundness, market pressures may force an expansion to specific financial privacy concerns.

PART FOUR

CONSUMER PERCEPTIONS OF FINANCIAL PRIVACY

Focus of Study

Part one analyzed privacy as a global issue and identified the impact of the European Union Data Protection Directive. Part two reviewed the current legislative and regulatory initiatives in the United States, as well as, discussed the political landscape of the privacy issue. Part three reviewed the specific privacy activity within the financial sector. Part four will expand on current privacy research in the financial services sector.

The focus of the study is to explore, describe and assess the privacy concerns of today's consumer, as well as determine the potential impact of consumer privacy concerns on technological innovation and public policy. The study builds on current quantitative research on privacy in the financial services sector. The project will expand the research conducted by Yankelovich Partners in 1994, the 1996 Equifax-Harris Consumer Privacy Survey, and the 1998 Privacy Concerns & Consumer Choice Survey. This study will use a qualitative approach to determine financial privacy attitudes and perspectives of professionals of color.

Research Question

This study began by asserting that consumer attitudes would ultimately form privacy operational standards. I have narrowed the focus to examine the foundation of operational standards of African American professionals. This group is the focus of the research. The question is how can consumer concepts of privacy be utilized to guide electronic commerce, public policy, and develop financial education for under represented populations as a public affairs initiative.

Literature Review

Although financial privacy attitudes and perceptions of people of color have not been studied in a scholarly context, quantitative surveys on consumer perceptions can be found. Yankelovich Partners took an in-depth look at privacy in a national study of 507 randomly selected respondents. Data was gathered by 25 minute telephone interviews between May 13 and May 22, 1994. Respondents were 18 to 54 years of age, with a household income of at least $18,000.

The Yankelovich Study revealed that seventy-five percent of consumers polled agree: "We need to find ways to stop business and government from collecting so much information about the average person." Consumers in the survey believed that the collection of data on personal behavior is unacceptable. This includes telephone numbers called (at home and at work), purchases made on credit cards, family information, video rentals, prescription drugs purchased, and medical history. Although in certain circumstances, it is acceptable to collect information. This is especially true of information that companies, government, or others may have a specific reason to process. For example, name, date of birth, and videotaping at ATM machines are considered the most acceptable. A clear majority of consumers polled believe information collected about them and their families is used for intended purposes only. Conversely, among those who sense the boundaries are not so clearly defined, seventy-five percent believe the use of information beyond intended purposes is a violation of confidentiality. ("Balancing the Power of Information", Privacy Study, Yankelovich Partners, 1994)

The 1996 Equifax-Harris Consumer Privacy Survey explored the degree to which consumers find certain practices acceptable. For example, the survey examined consumer attitudes about the use of information in credit reporting, insurance prescreening, credit scoring, medical data for general healthcare research, as well as on the Internet and Online services. The results of the 1996 Equifax-Harris Consumer Privacy Survey are based on 1,005 telephone interviews conducted July 20-29, 1996. All interviewing took place with adults 18 years and older, representing a cross-section of adults in the 48 contiguous United States. Completed interviews were weighed according to age, education, race, and sex to bring the sample profile in line with the overall profile of adults in the forty-eight states. (1996 Equifax-Harris Consumer Privacy Survey, October 8, 1996)

The Equifax Survey revealed that nearly two-thirds of the public say "protecting the privacy of consumer information" is "very" important to them. This figure represents a significant four-point increase since 1995 when sixty-one percent expressed a similar feeling. Twenty-four percent of the respondents have personally experienced a privacy invasion. The survey further revealed that public opinion is divided regarding privacy protection on the Internet, with Internet users leaning toward greater privacy protection and less intervention on the part of the government. (1996 Equifax-Harris Consumer Privacy, October 8, 1996)

Consumer Apprehensions

The 1998 Privacy Concerns & Consumer Choice Survey is based on interviews with a national cross-section of 1,008 adults, 18 years of age and older. All interviews were conducted by telephone from June 23 to July 16, 1998. The survey revealed that concerns over threats to personal privacy remain very high and in some cases are increasing. In addition, most people feel that businesses ask for too much personal information, and that consumers have lost control over how this information is used. As a result, consumers are refusing to give certain information to businesses at an increasing rate. Either through direct experience with a privacy invasion or as a result of generalized concerns about personal privacy, 78 percent say they have refused to give information to a business because they thought it was not really needed or was too personal. The findings also revealed that 43 percent of consumers have asked a business to withhold their name and address from a list that is sold or shared with other companies. This demonstrates consumer desire to gain control of personal information. (1998 Privacy Concerns & Consumer Choice, November 18, 1998.)

Group Perceptions

The most revealing and relevant result of the 1998 Privacy Concerns & Consumer Choice Survey is the demographic group findings. The findings are somewhat contradictory and offer no clear explanation. According to the survey:

Hispanics and African-Americans are much less critical than Whites when it comes to their opinions of privacy protection and business practices.

Hispanics are among those most likely to report having been victimized by a privacy invasion.

Hispanics and African-Americans also are much more likely than Whites to say they've noticed that businesses are paying more attention to privacy issues these days, and Hispanics (in particular) are less likely to think businesses ask for too much information (38% v. 57% for African-Americans and 48% for Whites).

Hispanics also are more likely to agree that their rights to privacy as a consumer are protected. Specifically, 51% of Hispanics agree that their rights to privacy are protected v. 42% among African-Americans and 36% among Whites.

Relatively few participants have purchased goods or services through the Internet. Specifically, only 31% of those surveyed report that they or some member of the household has made a purchase through the Internet. Interest is relatively low among consumers who are concerned about privacy and to some extent among those who feel they have been victimized in the past.

Methodology

The study expanded on the existing quantitative research conducted by Yankelovich Partners, Equifax-Harris, and Harris-Westin, with a qualitative analysis. In keeping with the original research, focus groups were used to understand attitudes, beliefs, practices and values. This methodology offers a viable supplement to quantitative sample surveys and appropriately supplements quantitative analysis of consumer privacy.

Four focus group discussions were conducted in the fall of 1998. These sessions were recorded verbatim. The first group consisted of a random sample of college students in Hartford, Connecticut. The second group was a sample of convenience with participants from the Mid-Atlantic region of the country. The third and fourth groups were randomly selected from Fairfield County chapter membership lists of an African-American community organization and an African-American fraternity.

The focus groups were held in the evenings at 12 Main Street, Anytown, USA. Benjamin Robinson moderated the groups and Danyelle Williams served as the assistant moderator. The sessions were pre-planned and lasted approximately ninety minutes.

The findings of all focus group sessions were video recorded. The transcript contains only comments that directly relate to financial privacy and a summary of the comments. For clarity, all quotes are verbatim with paraphrases enclosed in brackets.

The data is compared and contrasted according to perceptions and concerns of participants' privacy experiences and general knowledge of privacy in banking and finance. The following references were used for additional analysis:

Jane T. Bertrand, Judith E. Brown and Victoria M. Ward, "*Techniques forAnalyzing Focus Group Data,*" Evaluation Review, April 1992, 198.

Bertrand et al., "Techniques for Analyzing," 1992.

Richard A. Kruger, Focus Groups: A Practical Guide for Applied Research-second edition, 1994.

Findings

I.   Banking, Finance, and Privacy Attitudes

A.   What concerns you most about the protection of your personal information? Why? Anything else?

How much of one's life is private? (Mildred, Oct. 10)

The number of phone calls received from marketers. (Frances, Oct.10)

Some things should be kept private. (Vince, Oct. 10)

Mail and the availability of info through mailings. (Stan, Oct. 10)

Making mistakes with information that has been obtained. (Cheryl, Oct. 15)

Having access to information that should be private. (Cheryl, Oct. 15)

People can find out information about you and no one knows the source in which they obtained the information. (Bernicestine)

Who has access to our information and what can be done with it. (Chris, Oct. 16)

The increased amount of information available. (Leo, Oct. 16)

B.   Of all these concerns, prioritize what you are most and least concerned about relative to your banking and financial life.

My financial or net worth {most concerned}. (Frances, Oct. 10)
Who has access {most concerned} and the use of the unauthorized information {least concerned}. (Mildred, Oct. 10)
Manipulating and hacking {most concerned}. (Vince, Oct. 10)
Notification of credit checks {most concerned}. (Frances, Oct. 10)
Another state in which I live knowing financial information about me {most concerned}. (Stan, Oct. 10)
Purchasing prices of homes and rates {most concerned}. (Eugenia, Oct. 15)
Control over what is released {most concerned}. (Cheryl, Oct. 15)
Security {most concerned}, access, use and amount {least concerned}. (Leo, Oct. 16)

C. What personal information do you give out without concern for your privacy? How do you feel about the access to that information?
I give out my social security number. (Stan, Oct. 10)
I give out my name, address and business telephone number. (Frances, Oct. 10)
I will give out my social security number, driver's license, date of birth, work telephone number and personal geographic information. (Ronald, Oct. 16)
The more critical the information is to my privacy, the more reluctant I am to make it available. (Christopher, Oct. 16)

D. You are aware of the current situation with the President of the United States. Although there are many interesting issues, please focus on the issue of personal privacy. What are your feelings on the President of the United States and the right or privilege of personal privacy?
The President should be allowed some private life. (Vince, Oct. 10)
He deserves privacy and the deposition should not have been publicized. (Cheryl, Oct. 10)
He should have some degree of privacy. (Frances, Oct. 10)

Although he still has an obligation to the country, he should still be allowed a private life. (Stan, Oct. 10)

There is a fine line regarding privacy. There have been other unethical issues in the past relating to government officials, as well, and we seem to pick and choose public or private issues. He is entitled to a private life. (Ed, Oct. 15)

This issue that has been going on about the President should have been worked out before it reached the people. (Cheryl, Oct. 15)

{Yes, the President should have a private life.} (Leo, Leah, Christopher & Ronald, Oct. 15)

He has a right to privacy even when he is "on call." (Leah, Oct. 16)

Everyone needs a certain amount of privacy. (Leo, Oct. 16)

Celebrities have a "different" or "public" type of privacy. (Christopher, Oct. 16)

II.   Reaction to General Privacy Issues

A.   How important is the security of your banking and financial transactions?

I am least concerned about my privacy as long as there is no strict invasion. If I know it is secure, I'm less concerned about the privacy. (Shawn, Oct. 15)

There should be a choice on what information is given. (Cheryl, Oct. 15)

My banking and financial transactions and banking are very important. (Christopher, Oct. 16)

B.   Have you personally ever been the victim of what you felt was an improper invasion of privacy, or not? If yes, how did you feel?

Yes I have. It took some time before the situation was cleared up. (Frances, Oct. 10)

Yes I have. (Christopher, Oct. 16)

The more violations that take place, the more desensitized you become. (Christopher, Oct. 16)

You become increasingly agitated with situations regarding violation and the Internet. (Christopher, Oct 16)

C.   Was that improper invasion of your privacy carried out by the government, by a business, by an individual, or by some other source? {Business.} (Christopher & Ronald, Oct. 16)

D.   The present system in the United States for protecting the confidentiality of consumer information used by businesses combines three main controls: voluntary privacy practices adopted by companies, individual lawsuits and court decisions, and federal and state laws in specific industries. Some experts feel Congress should create a permanent federal government Privacy Commission, as some European countries have done. This Commission would examine new technology development and could issue and enforce privacy regulations governing all business in the United States. Other experts believe the present system is flexible enough to apply those consumer privacy rights that the American public wants to have protected, and that creating a federal Commission gives too much authority to the federal government. What do you feel about government involvement?

The average person could not understand that type of system. There would have to be some type of education for people to learn the rules and regulations. (Stan, Oct. 10)

In order the government to guard privacy, they would have to know what it [the private information] is. Technology could also be used to help with the protection of privacy. (Vince, Oct. 10)

I would not trust the government's involvement. (Cheryl, Oct. 15)

The setting of guidelines would be helpful. Power is present [for government] to invade privacy.

III. The Use of Consumer Information

A. How do you feel about current use of personal information by businesses?

I don't care for information to be passed along to others, but it can be beneficial when looking for useful information. (Frances, Oct. 10)

Businesses target certain people within the household whom they know will be interested in buying their product or services. (Stan, Oct. 10)

I would rather seek out information than have someone call me with offers. (Cheryl, Oct. 10)

I am appalled. (Christopher, Oct. 16)

I have a concern about access and use of information. (Leo, Oct. 16)

B. Have you ever refused to give personal information to businesses? What was the outcome and how did you feel?

I refused to give information when I thought it was not necessary for them to know. (Cheryl, Oct. 10)

I felt a sense of power when I refused to give information. (Eugenia, Oct. 15) There was a sense of power when I didn't give out information. (Ronald, Oct. 16)

C. As technology advances, the use of personal consumer information will become more accessible. To what extent are you comfortable with the sharing of your personal information in an evolving information age?

My anxiety increases with the advancement of technology. (Cheryl, Oct. 15)

I'm less concerned about the evolution of the technological age because of the ways I can remedy invasions. (Ed, Oct 15)

D. How do you feel about the use of information in an effort to provide security to banking and financial transactions?

The more specified access there is to information and the more personalized it is, the better. (Cheryl, Oct. 10)

Giving information is fine but the unauthorized release of information should be able to be prosecuted. (Cheryl, Oct. 15)

Benefit is also an issue when releasing information. Will the release of certain information serve some purpose or benefit me in the end. (Shawn, Oct. 15)

I agree that with the more information that is released, the less secure it becomes. (Leo, Oct. 16)

IV. Credit Reports

A. What is your feeling about credit reports?
They are inaccurate, confuse names and social security numbers. (Frances, Oct. 10)
Credit reports are excellent to use to evaluate credit. (Vince, Oct. 10)
They are hard to read and understand. (Frances, Oct. 10)

B. Have you ever had a negative experience with the use of information from a credit report?
Yes I have. It took a long time to clear up the problem. (Frances, Oct. 10)

C. How do you feel about the use of credit reports to determine credit worthiness?
They are necessary because there needs to be some standard. (Leo, Oct. 16)
It is unfair to have unused credit factored into credit worthiness. (Christopher, Oct. 16)
There is bias when it comes to evaluating males and females on credit worthiness. (Cheryl, Oct. 15)

V. Banking, Finance and Technology

A. Consumers are advised to check their credit reports before any major purchase, such as a mortgage, auto loan, or special credit card application. This is to make sure that all the information in the report is accurate and complete, and to explain any unusual items to potential credit grantors. How interested would you be in a computer-based on-line service that allows you to access your credit report with the use of an ID and password? Does this pose any concern for security or privacy?

> This could cause a problem for many people. (Mildred, Oct. 10)
> I think it would be a good idea. (Ed, Oct. 15)
> I'm not sure how I feel about that. (Cheryl, Oct. 15)
> Absolutely! (Leah, Oct. 16)

VI. Susceptibility and Internet Concerns

A. Given your experiences as an African-American, are people of color more susceptible to invasions of privacy?
Yes. (Vince, Cheryl, Mildred, Stan & Frances, Oct. 10)
{That is clearly the case.} (Shawn, Ed, Cheryl, Bernestine & Eugenia, Oct. 15)
No. (Leo, Christopher, Ronald & Leah, Oct. 16)

B. What is your feeling of using the Internet to purchase goods and services?
{I would not purchase anything over the Internet.} (All responded)

Summary of Themes

In each group session, the participants cited a number of factors on financial privacy with three characteristics mentioned as most critical. These were a lack of control of information being collected and used, increased concern as technology evolves, and discomfort in governmental protection. As technology advances and the use of personal consumer information becomes more accessible, participants believe protection of personal privacy will become more difficult. The increased difficulty of privacy protection is further complicated by the lack of confidence in government regulation of the private sector. Effective safeguards can not be achieved due to the technology gap between the government and the business industry. This gap will widen as the information age evolves.

Lack of Control of Information

Participants were most concerned about the availability, access, and accuracy of personal information. Individuals had similar concerns about banking and financial information, although the focus was on inappropriate marketing use of the information. The security of personal financial information allowed for increased levels of privacy tolerance to protect the information. While security use of personal information tends to be acceptable, the marketing use of specific financial information is largely unacceptable.

Participants felt comfortable giving less critical information, but in practice give social security number, name, address driver's license, and business telephone number without regard for privacy invasions. Many felt that divulging these types of personal data were necessary to complete transactions.

Security of banking and financial transactions is more important than invasions of privacy. Consistent with such attitudes, participants consider financial institutions responsible for the security of banking and financial transactions and perceive marketing of such information as misuse. On the other hand, a few participants were unfamiliar with the practice of financial information being used for marketing purposes.

Increased Concern as Technology Evolves

As technology advances and the use of personal consumer information becomes more accessible, participants believe protection of personal privacy will become more difficult. A computer-based on-line service that allows you to access your credit report would ultimately subject consumers to more invasions of privacy with potentially damaging outcomes to security and eventually creditworthiness.

Discomfort in Governmental Protection

Within the context of an improper invasion of privacy, participants become more desensitized as perceived violations of privacy increase. On the basis of such attitudes, individuals can be viewed as more apathetic and tolerant of invasions of privacy as incidents occur. This attitude can remain dormant until an individual becomes aware, perhaps from a privacy violation incident, of personal rights afforded by U.S. laws.

Most improper invasions of privacy were carried out by the business industry. Participants viewed the present system in the United States for protecting the confidentiality of consumer information used by businesses as inadequate. However, the U.S. government is incapable of regulating the private sector due to the technology gap between the government and the business industry. A permanent federal government Privacy Commission would be ineffective.

With minimum exceptions, participants believe that people of color are more susceptible to invasions of privacy and that the evolution of the information age will increase the vulnerability of people. All individuals responded that they would not use the Internet to purchase goods and services. The apathy to utilize electronic commerce is the result of the vulnerability and privacy tolerance of people of color. Use of the Internet to purchase goods and services gives the consumer the power of choice. The focus group participants feel less vulnerable by not conducting transactions via the Internet.

Conclusions

No studies to date have thoroughly investigated the financial privacy concerns of people of color. Current quantitative studies assert that certain underrepresented groups exhibit a lack of concern about financial privacy, have a higher incidence of perceived privacy invasions, and feel that their financial privacy is protected. However, a qualitative analysis found evidence in the contrary. People of color are very concerned and critical about financial privacy protection and business practices. Their concerns are focused on the access of information and the unauthorized use of specific information. As privacy invasions occur, people of color are desensitized to the violations and become tolerant to the collection and use of personal information. The tolerance is consistent with the history of powerlessness among people of color. People of color have a higher sense of vulnerability and feel less capable of protecting financial privacy.

There is an overall lack of confidence regarding the government's ability to protect consumer privacy in the information age. For people of color, the practice of purchasing goods and services via the Internet is consistent with the general population. The concern for privacy protection has stifled electronic commerce growth for all demographic groups. Consumer concepts of privacy must be managed from an educational perspective to gain consumer comfort and acceptance with electronic commerce. Public policy must be based on actual consumer attitudes as opposed to theory of effective legislation.

Finally, the findings of this study would suggest that the past quantitative approaches do not accurately reflect the feelings and attitudes of underrepresented populations. The strength of the qualitative findings warrants further research. The findings of this study have implications for consumer education. The study confirmed a need to educate according to cultural perceptions of privacy. As government attempts to refine principles and introduce the nine specific characteristics of effective self-regulation for privacy (awareness, choice, data security, data integrity, consumer access, accountability, consumer recourse, verification and consequences), the cultural perceptions of privacy can be used to develop better privacy principles in the information age. As government creates safe harbors for the private sector, the need for effective and inclusive consumer education becomes more imperative. In the future, effective and inclusive consumer education will begin to correct deficit privacy conditions for children of color.

Limitations and Suggestions for Further Research

Further research efforts in the area of privacy need to investigate the cultural perceptions of privacy. Consumer vulnerability and privacy tolerance of people of color has a significant impact on electronic commerce. In addition, the changing demographics of communities as it relates to privacy warrant additional research.

The exploratory nature of the present study involved the use of a sample of professionals of color. Future studies should attempt to choose samples that improve the finding's generalizability for an international community of individuals from different generations. Longitudinal studies that track attitudes and beliefs on privacy will be invaluable. Cross-sectional research which compares younger individuals of color to mature individuals of color would also provide important insight into the question of whether these perceptions and attitudes is generational, developmental, and/or educational.

The validity of demographic concentration must also be investigated using other regions of the country. Although the sample provided individuals born in different regions of the country, all participants reside in the Northeast region of the United States. The sample's response to several questions may be a function of their proximity to major corporate centers with easier access to information on financial privacy. It will be important to track the perceptions and attitudes of individuals in more rural regions of the country.

Lastly, the relationship found between familiarity with technology and perceptions of financial security suggests that research should be focussed in this area. Examining how and why different segments use technology will be helpful in better understanding electronic commerce. The effectiveness of different educational programs designed to teach the use of technology must also be assessed. Does awareness of technology foster the use of electronic commerce? The role of computer knowledge in the evolving information age also requires further investigation.

APPENDICES

Appendix A

Operational Definition of Terms

Asset-anything with monetary value owned by an individual.

Credit report-detailed report furnished by a credit-reporting agency to determine an individual's credit and financial history.

Creditworthiness-general qualification for borrowing from a financial institution or other credit source.

Debt level-total amount of an individual's financial obligations.
Bankrupt-state of being unable to repay financial obligations and debts as they come due or liabilities exceed assets.

Delinquent-state of being unable to pay a financial obligation when due.

Credit risk-assessment of an individual's ability to repay a financial obligation.

Financial life-the on going management of money, assets, and liabilities.

Information age-period where technology and the use of computers dominates the lives of every individual.

Internet -evolving medium that utilizes cyberspace to conduct commerce and transfer information via the computer.

Invasion of privacy-unwanted or unsuspected access of personal information.

Liability-an obligation to repay a debt.

People of color-group of individuals identified by a particular socio-economic level, cultural identity, and differential treatment by society.

Personal information-information pertaining to a particular person's affairs.
Personal privacy-the management and use of personal information.

Security-the protection of personal information.

Spending patterns-identified habits of using money or credit to purchase goods and services

APPENDIX B

Focus Group Sessions

I. PILOT, Thursday, September 10, 1998,
American National Government Class, Hartford, Connecticut

Saturday, October 10, 1998

Participant Age	Occupation	Highest Education	#Children	Salary (000's)
1) South Jersey 53	Medical Consultant	Graduate School	1	
2) South Jersey 72	Dentist	Dental School	3	
3) Philadelphia 60	Physician	Medical School	2	
4) Sicklerville, NJ 55	MIS Manager	Bachelor's Degree	2	
5) Sicklerville, NJ 53	Special Ed. Teacher	Bachelor's Degree	1	

Thursday, October 15, 1998

6) Westport, CT	Consultant	Bachelor's Degree	2	150+
7) Westport, CT 40s	Entrepreneur	Bachelor's Degree	2	0-40
8) Norwalk, CT 28	Financial Sales	Law School	2	70-90
9) Norwalk, CT 36	Telecom Sales	Bachelor's Degree	1	
10) Westport, CT 50	Executive Assistant	Bachelor's Degree	2	110-150

Friday, October 16, 1998

11) Norwalk, CT 48	Registered Nurse	Master's Degree	2	110-150
12) Norwalk, CT 57	Banker	Master's Degree	2	110-150
13) Norwalk, CT 32	Sales Manager	Master's Degree	2	110-150
14) New Haven, CT 42	State Employee	Master's Degree	2	90-110

Appendix C

Focus Group Agenda

I.   Introduction (10 minutes)

A. Moderator introduction
B. Purpose of the focus groups
C. Explanation of the setup, disclosure (video taping), and assurance of confidentiality.
D. Respondents introduce themselves (name, address, occupation, children, educational background)

II.   Warm-Up On Banking, Finance and Privacy Attitudes (10 minutes)

A. What concerns you most about the protection of your personal information? Why? Anything else?
B. Of all these concerns, prioritize what you are most and least concerned about relative to your banking and financial life.
C. What personal information do you give out without concern for your privacy? How do you feel about the access to that information?
D. You are aware of the current situation with the President of the United States. Although there are many interesting issues, please focus on the issue of personal privacy. What are your feelings on the President of the United States and the right or privilege of personal privacy?

III. **Reaction to General Privacy Issues (15 minutes)**

A. How important is the security of your banking and financial transactions?

B. Have you personally ever been the victim of what you felt was an improper invasion of privacy, or not? If yes, how did you feel?

C. Was that improper invasion of your privacy carried out by the government, by a business, by an individual, or by some other source?

D. The present system in the United States for protecting the confidentiality of consumer information used by businesses combines three main controls: voluntary privacy practices adopted by companies, individual lawsuits and court decisions, and federal and state laws in specific industries. Some experts feel Congress should create a permanent federal government Privacy Commission, as some European countries have done. This Commission would examine new technology development and could issue and enforce privacy regulations governing all business in the United States. Other experts believe the present system is flexible enough to apply those consumer privacy rights that the American public wants to have protected, and that creating a federal Commission gives too much authority to the federal government. What do you feel about government involvement?

IV. **The Use of Consumer Information (15 minutes)**

A. How do you feel about current use of personal information by businesses?

B. Have you ever refused to give personal information to businesses? What was the outcome and how did you feel?

C. As technology advances, the use of personal consumer information will become more accessible. To what extent are you comfortable with the sharing of your personal information in an evolving information age?

D. How do you feel about the use of information in an effort to provide security to banking and financial transactions?

V. Credit Reports (15 minutes)

A. What is your feeling about credit reports?

B. Have you ever had a negative experience with the use of information from a credit report?

C. How do you feel about the use of credit reports to determine creditworthiness?

D. Businesses that grant credit use formulas from credit reporting companies to identify customers whose debt levels and spending patterns strongly suggest they will go bankrupt or become seriously delinquent. These businesses use these formulas to determine whether a customer is a good credit risk. What is your feeling of this practice?

VI. Banking, Finance and Technology (10 minutes)

A. Consumers are advised to check their credit reports before any major purchase, such as a mortgage, auto loan, or special credit card application. This is to make sure that all the information in the report is accurate and complete, and to explain any unusual items to potential credit grantors. How interested would you be in a computer-based on-line service that allows you to access your credit report with the use of an ID and password? Does this pose any concern for security or privacy?

VII. Wrap-up

A. Given your experiences as an African-American, are people of colormore susceptible to invasions of privacy?

B. What is your feeling of using the Internet to purchase goods and services?

APPENDIX D

Participant Letter

October 11, 1998

Ms. Jane Participant
123 Main Street
Anytown, CT 12345

Dear Ms. Participant:

Thank you for accepting my invitation to attend the discussion on privacy. The reception and discussion will take place at 12 Main Street in Anytown, USA on **Friday, October xx, 1998 at 6:30 p.m.** Enclosed, please find directions for your use. The discussion will begin promptly at 7:00 p.m. Food and refreshments will be available throughout the evening.

The research study will use a qualitative model to gather comprehensive depictions or descriptions of your experience. In this way, I hope to answer my question: How can consumer concepts of privacy be utilized to guide electronic commerce, public policy, and develop financial education for under represented populations as a public affairs initiative?

Consumer protection and privacy are emerging as essential issues in the financial services sector. Improvements in the rapid transfer of information provide a new medium for the purchase of goods and services, that is, the medium of electronic commerce. Consumer privacy deals with how and what types of information are collected and how the data is utilized. My dissertation assesses the privacy concerns of today's consumer, as well as determines the potential impact of consumer privacy concerns on technological innovation and public policy.

Through your participation, I hope to understand the essence of privacy as it reveals itself in your experience. You will participate in a discussion to understand your attitudes, beliefs, practices and values on privacy. I will be looking for patterns in your responses and will use some of your responses as examples. I am not aware of any risks involved in participation in this study. You are free to decline to participate or withdraw at any time.

I thank you for your consideration and commitment of time, energy and effort. I look forward to seeing you on October xx. If you have any questions or concerns, please contact me at (123) 456-7890.

Sincerely,

Benjamin E. Robinson III
Doctoral Candidate
The Union Graduate School

Enclosures: Participant-Release Agreement
             Directions

APPENDIX E

Laws addressing financial privacy

◆ *The Fair Credit Reporting Act of 1970* (FCRA), I 5 U.S.C. § *1681 et seq.,* governs the information practices of consumer reporting agencies, such as credit bureaus, and the use of consumer reports and the sharing of affiliate information by financial institution holding companies and other multicompany organizations. These information-sharing rules contemplate notice to consumers and an opportunity to opt-out of such sharing.

◆ *The Electronic Fund Transfer Act of 1978,* 15 U.S.C. § 1693 *et seq.,* provides a basic framework establishing the rights, liabilities and responsibilities of parties to electronic fund transfers. Though its primary objective is to protect the rights of individuals who transfer funds electronically, it also requires notice by financial institutions of the circumstances when account information will be disclosed to third parties.

◆ *The Fair Debt Collection Practices Act,* 15 U.S.C. § 1601 *et seq.,* prohibits excessive and abusive collection practices and essentially limits intrusion on consumers' privacy in collectors' contacts with debtors. This was enacted to protect the privacy of debtors.

◆ *The Fair Credit Billing Act* (FCBA), 15 U.S.C. § 1666 *et seq.,* creates a statutory right to challenge the accuracy of information contained in the creditor's file.

◆   *The Telephone Consumer Protection Act of 1991*, 47 U.S.C. § 227, governs telephone solicitations and grants rulemaking authority to the Federal Communications Commission to prescribe regulations necessary to protect residential subscribers' privacy rights for avoiding telephone solicitations to which they object.

◆   *The Telemarketing and Consumer Fraud and Abuse Prevention Act of 1991*, 15 U.S.C. § 6101 *et seq.*, protects consumers against deceptive and abusive telemarketing for the sale of goods and services by creating a civil cause of action and money damages for violations. It also permits states to bring enforcement actions.

◆   *The Federal Trade Commission Act* as amended, 15 U.S.C. § 41 *et seq.*, requires each of the federal bank supervisory agencies to establish a separate division of consumer affairs to handle consumer complaints regarding unfair or deceptive acts or practices. In addition to complaints regarding violations of existing law, a complaint can be directed at an act or practice even if it is expressly authorized or not prohibited by current law. It can also be used to enforce an institution's disclosed privacy principles. For financial institutions, compliance is enforced under *The Federal Deposit Insurance Act*. 12 U.S.C. § 1818.

◆   *The Right to Financial Privacy Act of 1978*, 12 U.S.C. § 3401 *et seq.*, was enacted as a direct response to the *United States v. Miller* decision, and established notice and procedures for access to financial information by federal government agencies. The same is true of the corresponding provisions of the tax law governing IRS access to financial records. I.R.C.§§ 7609-761 0.

◆   *The Electronic Communications Privacy Act of 1986,* 18 U.S.C. § 2510 *et seq.*, is intended to protect against unauthorized interception of electronic communications.

◆ *The Cable Communications Policy Act of 1984*, 47 U.S.C. § 551 *et seq.*, as amended by *The Cable Television Consumer Protection and Competition Act of 1992*, establishes written consumer disclosure requirements regarding the collection and use of personally identifiable information, prohibits the sharing of such information without the prior written or electronic consent of the customer. It further provides for access for customer inspection and error correction of information that is collected.

◆ *The Comprehensive Crime Control Act of 1984*, 18U.S.C. §1030 *et seq*, makes it a federal crime to access certain computer systems and obtain information without authorization. Congress elected to limit the focus to computer systems involving a compelling federal interest, such as computers maintained by the federal government and computers maintained by federally insured financial institutions.

(Source: Financial Privacy In America, A Review of Consumer Financial Services Issues, June, 1998)

Appendix F

European Union
The Council
Brussels, 2 February 1995
12003/1/95
Rev 1
Restreint
ECO 291
CODEC 92

Common Position (EC) No /95
Adopted by the Council on 20 February 1995
With a View to Adopting
Directive 94/ /EC of the European Parliament and of the Council
on the Protection of Individuals
With Regard to the Processing of Personal Data
And on the Free Movement of Such Data
Directive 95/ /EC of the European Parliament and of the Council
of
On the protection of individuals with regard to the processing of
personal data and on the free movement of such data

The European Parliament and the Council of the European Union,
Having regard to the Treaty establishing the European Community,
and in particular Article 100a thereof,
Having regard to the proposal from the Commission ([1]),

Having regard to the Opinion of the Economic and Social Committee ([2]),

Acting in accordance with the procedure referred to in Article 189b of the Treaty ([3]),

Whereas the objectives of the Community, as laid down in the Treaty, as amended by the Treaty on European Union, include establishing an ever closer union among the people of Europe, fostering closer relations between the States belonging to the Community, ensuring economic and social progress by common action to eliminate the barriers which divide Europe, encouraging the constant improvement of the living conditions of its people, preserving and strengthening peace and liberty and promoting democracy on the basis of the fundamental rights recognized in the constitutions and laws of the Member States and in the European Convention for the Protection of Human Rights and Fundamental Freedoms;

Whereas data-processing systems are designed to serve man; whereas they must, whatever the nationality or residence of natural persons, respect the fundamental freedoms and rights of individuals, notably the right to privacy, and contribute to economic and social progress, trade expansion and the well-being of individuals;

Whereas the establishment and functioning of an internal market in which, in accordance with Article 7a of the Treaty, the free movement of goods, persons, services and capital is ensured require not only that personal data should be able to flow freely from one Member State to another, but also that the fundamental rights of individuals should be safeguarded.

Whereas increasingly frequent recourse is being had in the Community to the processing of personal data in the various spheres of economic and social activity; whereas the progress made in information technology is making the processing and exchange of such data considerably easier;

Whereas the economic and social integration resulting from the establishment and functioning of the internal market within the meaning of Article 7a of the Treaty will necessarily lead to a substantial increase in cross-border flows of personal data between all those involved in a private or public capacity in economic and social activity in the Member States; whereas the exchange of personal data between undertakings in different Member States is set to increase; whereas the national authorities in the various Member States are being called upon by virtue of Community law to collaborate and exchange personal data so as to be able to perform their duties or carry out tasks on behalf of an authority in another Member State within the context of the area without internal frontiers as constituted by the Internal Market;

Whereas, furthermore, the increase in scientific and technical cooperation and the coordinated introduction of new telecommunications networks in the Community necessitate and facilitate cross-border flows of personal data;

Whereas the difference in levels of protection of the rights and freedoms of individuals, notably the right to privacy, with regard to the processing of personal data afforded in the Member States may prevent the transmission of such data from the territory of one Member State to that of another Member State; whereas this difference may therefore constitute an obstacle to the pursuit of a number of economic activities at Community level, distort competition and impede authorities in the discharge of their responsibilities under Community law; whereas this difference in levels of protection is due to the existence of a wide variety of national laws, regulations and administrative provisions;

Whereas, in order to remove the obstacles to flows of personal data, the level of protection of the rights and freedoms of individuals with regard to the processing of such data must be equivalent in all the Member States; whereas this objective is vital to the internal market but cannot be achieved by Member States alone, especially in view of the scale of the divergences which currently exist between the relevant laws in the Member States and the need to coordinate the laws of the Member States so as to ensure that the cross-border flow of personal data is regulated in a consistent manner that is in keeping with the objective of the internal market as provided for in Article 7a of the Treaty; whereas Community action to approximate those laws is therefore needed;

Whereas, given the equivalent protection resulting from the approximation of national laws, the Member States will no longer be able to inhibit the free movement between them of personal data on grounds relating to protection of the rights and freedoms of individuals, and in particular the right to privacy; whereas Member States will be left a margin for manoeuvre, which may, in the context of implementation of the Directive, also be exercised by the business and social partners; whereas Member States will therefore be able to specify in their national law the general conditions governing the lawfulness of data processing; whereas in doing so the Member States shall strive to improve the protection currently provided by their legislation; whereas, within the limits of this margin for manoeuvre and in accordance with Community law, disparities could arise in the implementation of the Directive, and this could have an effect on the movement of data within a Member State as well as within the Community;

Whereas the object of the national laws on the processing of personal data is to protect fundamental rights and freedoms, notably the right to privacy, which is recognized both in Article 8 of the European Convention for the Protection of Human Rights and Fundamental Freedoms and in the general principles of Community law; whereas, for that reason, the approximation of those laws must not result in any lessening of the protection they afford but must, on the contrary, seek to ensure a high level of protection in the Community;

Whereas the principles of the protection of the rights and freedoms of individuals, notably the right to privacy, which are contained in this

Directive, give substance to and amplify those contained in the Council of Europe Convention of 28 January 1981 for the Protection of Individuals with regard to Automatic Processing of Personal Data;

Whereas the protection principles must apply to all processing of personal data by any person whose activities are governed by Community law; whereas there should be excluded the processing of data carried out by a natural person in the exercise of activities which are exclusively personal or domestic, such as correspondence and the holding of records of addresses;

Whereas the activities referred to in Titles V and VI of the Treaty on European Union regarding public safety, defence, State security or the activities of the State in the area of criminal law fall outside the scope of Community law, without prejudice to the obligations incumbent upon Member States under Article 56(2), Article 57 or Article 100a of the Treaty establishing the European Community; whereas the processing of personal data that is necessary to safeguard the economic well-being of the State does not fall within the scope of this Directive where such processing relates to State security matters;

Whereas, given the importance of the developments under way, in the framework of the information society, of the techniques used to capture, transmit, manipulate, record, store or communicate sound and image data relating to natural persons, this Directive should be applicable to processing involving such data;

Whereas the processing of such data is covered by this Directive only if it is automated or if the data processed are contained or are intended to be contained in a filing system structured according to specific criteria relating to individuals, so as to permit easy access to the personal data in question;

Whereas the processing of sound and image data, such as in cases of video surveillance, does not come within the scope of this Directive if it is carried out for the purposes of public security, defence, national security or in the course of State activities relating to the area of criminal law or of other activities which do not come within the scope of Community law;

Whereas as far as the processing of sound and image data carried out for purposes of journalism or the purposes of literary or artistic expression is concerned, in particular in the audiovisual field, the principles of the Directive are to apply in a restricted manner according to the provisions laid down in Article 9,

Whereas, in order to ensure that individuals are not deprived of the protection to which they are entitled under this Directive, any processing of personal data in the Community must be carried out in accordance with the law of one of the Member States; whereas, in this connection, processing carried out under the responsibility of a controller who is established in a Member State should be governed by the law of that State;

Whereas establishment on the territory of a Member State implies the effective and real exercise of activity through the means of a stable set-up; whereas the legal form of such an establishment, whether a simple branch or a subsidiary with a legal personality, is not the determinate factor in this respect; whereas, when a single controller is established on the territory of several Member States, particularly be means of a subsidiary, he must ensure, in order to avoid any circumvention of national rules, that each of the establishments fulfils the obligations imposed by the national law applicable to its activities;

Whereas the fact that processing is carried out by a person established in a third country must not stand in the way of the protection of individuals provided for in this Directive; whereas, in these cases, the processing should be governed by the law of the Member State in which the means used are located, and there should be guarantees to ensure that the rights and obligations provided for in this Directive are respected in practice;

Whereas this Directive is without prejudice to the rules of territoriality applicable in criminal matters;

Whereas Member States shall more precisely define in the laws they enact or when bringing into force the measures taken under this Directive, the general circumstances in which processing is lawful; whereas in particular Article 5, in conjunction with Articles 7 and 8, allows Member States, independently of general rules, to provide for special processing conditions for specific sectors and for the various categories of data covered by Article 8;

Whereas Member States are empowered to ensure the implementation of the protection of individuals both by means of a general law on the protection of individuals against the processing of personal data and by sectorial laws such as those relating, for example, to Institutes for Statistics;

Whereas the legislation concerning the protection of legal persons with regard to the processing of data which concern them is not affected by this Directive;

Whereas the principles of protection must be reflected, on the one hand, in the obligations imposed on persons, public authorities, enterprises, agencies or other bodies responsible for processing, in particular regarding data quality, technical security, notification to the supervisory authority, and the circumstances under which processing can be carried out, and, on the other hand, in the rights conferred on individuals, the data on whom are the subject of processing, to be informed that processing is taking place, to consult the data, to request corrections and even to object to processing in certain circumstances;

Whereas the principles of protection must apply to any information concerning an identified or identifiable person; whereas, to determine whether a person is identifiable, account should be taken of all the means likely reasonably to be used either by the controller or by any other person to identify the said person; whereas the principles of protection shall not apply to data rendered anonymous in such a way that the data subject is no longer identifiable; whereas codes of conduct within the meaning of Article 27 may be a useful instrument in providing guidance as to the way in which data may be rendered anonymous and retained in a form in which identification of the data subject is no longer possible;

Whereas the protection of individuals must apply as much to automatic processing of data as to manual processing; whereas the scope of this protection must not in effect depend on the techniques used, otherwise this would create a serious risk of circumvention; whereas, nonetheless, as regards manual processing, this Directive covers only filing systems, not according to specific criteria relating to individuals allowing easy access to the personal data; whereas, in line with the definition in Article 2(c) the different criteria for determining the constituents of a structured set of personal data, and the different criteria governing access to such a set, can be laid down by each Member State; whereas files or sets of files as well as their cover pages, which are not structured according to specific criteria, shall under no circumstances fall within the scope of this Directive;

Whereas any processing of personal data must be lawful and fair to the individual concerned; whereas, in particular, the data must be adequate, relevant and not excessive in relation to the purposes for which they are processed; whereas such purposes must be explicit and legitimate and must be determined at the time of collection of the data; whereas the purposes of processing further to collection shall not be incompatible with the purposes as they were originally specified;

Whereas the further processing of personal data for historical, statistical, or scientific purposes is not generally to be considered incompatible with the purposes for which the data have previously been collected provided that Member States furnish suitable guarantees; whereas these guarantees must in particular rule out the use of data for taking measures or decisions regarding any particular individual;

Whereas, in order to be lawful, the processing of personal data must in addition be carried out with the consent of the data subject or be necessary with a view to the conclusion or performance of a contract binding on the data subject, or be required by law, by the performance of a task in the public interest or in the exercise of official authority, or by the interest of a natural or legal person provided that the interests or the rights and freedoms of the data subject are not overriding; whereas, in particular, in order to maintain a balance between the interests involved while guaranteeing effective competition, Member States remain free to determine the circumstances in which personal data may be used or disclosed to a third party in the context of the legitimate ordinary business activities of companies and other bodies; whereas Member States may similarly specify the conditions under which personal data may be disclosed to a third party for the purposes of marketing whether carried out commercially or b a charitable organization or by any other association or foundation, of a political nature for example, subject to the provisions allowing a data subject to object to the processing of data regarding him, at no cost and without having to state his reasons;

Whereas the processing of personal data must equally be regarded as lawful where it is carried out in order to protect an interest which is essential for the data subject's life;

Whereas it is for national legislation to determine whether the controller performing a task carried out in the public interest or in the exercise of official authority should be a public administration or another national or legal person governed by public law or by private law or such as a professional association;

Whereas data which are capable by their nature of infringing fundamental freedoms or privacy should not be processed unless the data subject gives his explicit consent; whereas, however, derogation from this prohibition must be explicitly provided for in respect of specific needs, in particular where the processing of these data is carried out for certain health-related purposes by individuals subject to a legal obligation of professional secrecy or in the course of legitimate activities by certain associations or foundations the purpose of which is to permit the exercise of fundamental freedoms;

Whereas Member States must Also be authorized, when justified by grounds of important public interest, to derogate from the prohibition on processing sensitive categories of data where important reasons of public interest so justify in areas such as public health and social protection, especially as regards the assurance of quality and cost-effectiveness, and as regards the procedures used for settling claims for benefits and services in the health insurance system, scientific research and government statistics; whereas it is incumbent on them, however, to provide specific and suitable safeguards so as to protect the fundamental rights and the privacy of individuals;

Whereas, moreover, the processing of personal data by official authorities for achieving aims, laid down in constitutional law or international public law, of officially recognized religious associations is carried out on important grounds of public interest;

Whereas where, in the course of electoral activities, the operation of the democratic system requires in certain Member States that political parties compile data on people's political opinions, the processing of such data can be permitted for reasons of important public interest, provided that appropriate safeguards are established;

Whereas the processing of personal data for purposes of journalism or for purposes of literary or artistic expression, in particular in the audiovisual field, should qualify for exemption from the requirements of certain provisions of this Directive insofar as this is necessary to reconcile the fundamental rights of individuals with freedom of information and notably the right to receive and impart information, as guaranteed in particular in Article 10 of the European Convention for the Protection of Human Rights and Fundamental Freedoms; whereas Member States should therefore lay down exemptions and derogations necessary for the purposes of balance between fundamental rights as regards general measures on the legitimacy of data processing, measures on the transfer of data to third countries and the powers of supervisory authority; whereas this should not, however, lead Member States to lay down exemptions from the measures to ensure security of processing; whereas the supervisory authority responsible for this sector should also be provided at least with certain ex-post powers, e.g. to publish a regular report or to refer matters to the judicial authorities;

Whereas, if the processing of data is to be fair, the data subject must be in a position to learn of the existence of a processing operation and, where data are collected from him, must be given accurate and full information, bearing in mind the circumstances of the collection;

Whereas certain processing operations involve data which the controller has not collected directly from the data subject; whereas, furthermore, data can be legitimately disclosed to a third party, even if the disclosure was not anticipated at the time the data were collected from the data subject; whereas, in all these cases, the data subject should be informed when the data are recorded or at the latest when the data are first disclosed to a third party;

Whereas, however, it is not necessary to impose this obligation if the data subject already knows the information; whereas, moreover, this obligation is not provided for if the recording or disclosure are expressly provided for by law or if the provision of information proves impossible or involved disproportionate efforts, which could be the case where processing is for historical, statistical or scientific purposes; whereas, in this regard, the number of data subjects, the age of the data, and any compensatory measures adopted may be taken into consideration;

Whereas any person must be able to exercise the right of access to data relating to him which are being processed, in order to verify in particular the accuracy of the data and the lawfulness of the processing; whereas, for the same reasons, every data subject must also have the right to know the logic involved in the automatic processing of data concerning him, at least in the case of the automated decisions referred to in Article 15(1); whereas this right must not be adversely affect business confidentiality or intellectual property and in particular the copyright protecting the software; whereas these considerations must not, however, result in the data subject being refused all information;

Whereas Member States may, in the interest of the data subject or so as to protect the rights and freedoms of others, restrict rights of access and information; whereas they may, for example, specify that access to medical data may be obtained only through a health professional;

Whereas restrictions on the rights of access and information and on certain obligations of the controller may similarly be imposed by Member States insofar as they are necessary to safeguard, for example, national security, defence, public safety, or important economic or financial interests of a Member State or the Union, as well as criminal investigations and prosecutions and action in respect of breaches of ethics in the regulated professions; whereas the list of exceptions and limitations should include the tasks of monitoring, inspection or regulation necessary in three last-mentioned areas concerning public security, economic or financial interests and crime prevention; whereas the listing of tasks in these three areas does not affect the legitimacy of exceptions or restrictions for reasons of State security or defence;

Whereas Member States may also be led, by virtue of the provisions of Community law, to derogate from the provisions of this Directive concerning the right of access, the obligation to inform individuals and the quality of data, in order to safeguard certain purposes among those referred to above;

Whereas, in cases of processing lawfully data pursued on grounds of public interest, official authority or the legitimate interests of a natural or legal person, any data subject should nevertheless be entitled, on legitimate and compelling grounds relating to his particular situation, to object to the processing of any data relating to himself; whereas

Member States nevertheless have the possibility of laying down national provisions to the contrary;

Whereas the protection of the rights and freedoms of data subjects with regard to the processing of personal data requires that appropriate technical and organizational measures be taken, both at the time of the design of the processing system and at the time of the processing itself, particularly in order to maintain security and thereby to prevent any unauthorized processing; whereas it is incumbent on the Member States to ensure that controllers comply with these measures; whereas these measures must ensure an appropriate level of security, taking into account the state of the technology and the cost of its use in view of the risks inherent in the processing and the nature of the data to be protected;

Whereas where a message containing personal data is transmitted by means of a telecommunications or electronic mail service, the sole purpose of which is the transmission of such messages, the controller in respect of the personal data contained in the message will normally be considered to be the person from whom the message originates, rather than the person offering the transmission services; whereas, nevertheless, those offering such services will normally be considered controllers in respect of the processing of the additional personal data necessary for the operation of the service;

Whereas the notification procedures are designed to ensure disclosure of the purposes and main features of any processing operation for the purpose of verification that the operation is in accordance with the national measures taken under this Directive;

Whereas, in order to avoid unsuitable administrative formalities, exemptions from the obligation to notify and simplification of the notification required may be provided for by Member States in cases where processing is unlikely to adversely affect the rights and freedoms of data subjects, provided that it is in accordance with a measure taken by a Member State specifying its limits; whereas in an equivalent way exemption or simplification can similarly be provided for by Member States where a person appointed by the controller ensures that the processing carried out is not likely adversely to affect the rights and freedoms of data subjects; whereas such an official, whether or not an employee of the controller, must be in a position to exercise his functions in complete independence;

Whereas exemption or simplification could be provided for in cases of processing operations whose sole purpose is the keeping of a register intended, according to national law, to provide information to the public and open to consultation by the public or by any person demonstrating a legitimate interest;

Whereas, nevertheless, simplification or exemption from the obligation to notify shall not release the controller from any of the other obligations resulting from this Directive;

Whereas, in this context, ex post facto verification by the competent authorities must be in general be considered a sufficient measure;

Whereas, however, certain processing operations are likely to pose specific risks to the rights and freedoms of data subjects by virtue of their nature, their scope or their purposes, such as the purpose of excluding individuals from a right, benefit or contract, or by virtue of the specific use of new technologies; whereas it is for Member States, if they so wish, to specify such risks in their legislation;

Whereas with regard to all the processing undertaken in society, the amount posing such specific risks should be very limited; whereas Member States must provide that the supervisory authority, or the data protection official in cooperation with the authority, check such processing prior to it being carried out; whereas following this prior check, the supervisory authority may, according to its national law, give an opinion or an authorization regarding the processing; whereas such checking may equally take place in the course of the preparation of a legislative measure adopted by the national parliament or on the basis of such a measure, defining the nature of the processing and specifying suitable safeguards;

Whereas, if the controller fails to respect the rights of data subjects, national legislation must provide for a judicial remedy; whereas any damage which a person may suffer as a result of unlawful processing must be compensated for by the controller, who may be exempted from liability if he proves that he is not responsible for the damage, in particular in cases where he reports an error on the part of the data subject or in a case of force majeure; whereas sanctions must be imposed on any person, whether governed by private or public law, who fails to comply with the national measures taken under this Directive;

Whereas cross-border flows of personal data are necessary to the expansion of international trade; whereas the protection of individuals guaranteed in the Community by this Directive does not stand in the way of transfers of personal data to third countries which ensure an adequate level of protection; whereas the adequacy of the level of protection afforded by a third country must be assessed in the light of all the circumstances surrounding the transfer operation or set of transfer operations;

Whereas, on the other hand, the transfer of personal data to a third country which does not ensure an adequate level of protection must be prohibited;

Whereas provision should be made for exemptions from this prohibition in certain circumstances where the data subject has given his consent, where the transfer is necessary in relation to a contract or a legal claim, where protection of an important public interest so requires, for example in cases of international transfers of data between tax or customs administrations or between services competent for social security matters, or where the transfer is made from a register established by law and intended for consultation by the public or persons having a legitimate interest; whereas in this case such a transfer should not involve the entirety of the data or entire categories of the data contained in the register and, when the register is intended for consultation by persons having a legitimate interest, the transfer should be made only at the request of the same persons or if the latter are the recipients;

Whereas particular measures may be taken to compensate for the lack of protection in a third country in cases where the person responsible for the processing offers appropriate assurances; whereas, moreover, provision must be made for procedures for negotiations between the Community and such third countries;

Whereas, in any event, transfers to third countries may only be effected in full compliance with the provisions adopted by the Member States pursuant to this Directive, and in particular Article 8 thereof;

Whereas Member States and the Commission, in their respective spheres of competence, must encourage the trade associations and other representative organizations concerned to draw up codes of conduct so far as to facilitate the application of this Directive, taking account of the specific characteristics of the processing carried out in certain sectors, and respecting the national provisions adopted for its implementation;

Whereas the establishment in Member States of supervisory authorities, exercising their functions with complete independence, is an essential component of the protection of individuals with regard to the processing of personal data;

Whereas such authorities must have the necessary means to perform their duties, including powers of investigation and intervention, particularly in cases of complaints from individuals, and powers to engage in legal proceedings; whereas such authorities must help to ensure transparency of processing in the Member States within those jurisdiction they fall;

Whereas the authorities in the different Member States will need to assist one another in performing their duties so as to ensure that the rules of protection are properly respected throughout the European Union;

Whereas, at Community level, a Working Party on the Protection of Individuals with regard to the Processing of Personal Data must be set up and be completely independent in the performance of its functions; whereas, having regard to its specific nature, it must advise the Commission and, in particular, contribute to the uniform application of the national rules adopted pursuant to this Directive;

Whereas, with regard to the transfer of data to third countries, the application of this Directive calls for the conferment of powers of implementation on the Commission and the establishment of a procedure in accordance with the procedures laid down in Council Decision 87/373/EEC(1)

Whereas the principles set out in this Directive regarding the protection of the rights and freedoms of individuals, notably their right to privacy, with regard to the processing of personal data may be supplemented or clarified, in particular as far as certain sectors are concerned, by specific rules based on those principles;

Whereas Member States should be allowed a period of not more than three years from the entry into force of the national measures transposing this Directive in which to apply such new national rules gradually to all processing operations already under way; whereas, in order to facilitate cost-efficient implementation, a further period expiring twelve years after the date on which this Directive is adopted will be allowed to Member States to ensure the conformity of existing manual filing systems with certain of the Directive's provisions; whereas data contained in such filing systems actively processed during this extended transition period should nevertheless be brought into conformity with these provisions at the time of such further active processing; Whereas an agreement on a "modus vivendi" between the European Parliament, the Council and the Commission concerning the implimenting measures for acts adopted in accordance with the procedure laid down in Article 189b of the EC Treaty was reached on 20 December 1994,

Whereas it is not necessary for the data subject to give his consent again so as to allow the controller to continue to process, after the national provisions taken pursuant to this Directive enter into force, any sensitive data necessary for the performance of a contract concluded on the basis of free and informed consent before the entry into force of these provisions;

Whereas this Directive does not stand in the way of a Member State's regulating marketing activities aimed at consumers residing in its territory insofar as much as such regulation does not concern the protection of individuals with regard to the processing of personal data;

Whereas the Directive allows the principle of public access to official documents to be taken into account when implementing the principles set out in this Directive,

HAVE ADOPTED THIS DIRECTIVE:

CHAPTER I

GENERAL PROVISIONS

Article 1

Object of the Directive

1. In accordance with this Directive, Member States shall protect the fundamental rights and freedoms of natural persons, and in particular their right to privacy, with respect to the processing of personal data.
2. Member States shall neither restrict nor prohibit the free flow of personal data between Member States for reasons connected with the protection afforded under paragraph 1.

Article 2 Definitions

For the purposes of this Directive:

(a) "personal data" shall mean any information relating to an identified or identifiable natural person ("data subject"); an identifiable person is one who can be identified, directly or indirectly, in particular by reference to an identification number or to one or more factors specific to his physical, physiological, mental, economic, cultural or social identity;
(b) "processing of personal data" ("processing") shall mean any operation or set of operations which is performed upon personal

data, whether or not by automatic means, such as collection, recording, organization, storage, adaptation or alteration, retrieval, consultation, use, disclosure by transmission, dissemination or otherwise making available, alignment or combination, blocking, erasure or destruction;

(c) "personal data filing system" ("filing system") shall mean any structured set of personal data which are accessible according to specific criteria, whether centralized, decentralized or dispersed on a functional or geographical basis;

(d) "controller" shall mean the natural or legal person, public authority, agency or any other body which alone or jointly with others determines the purposes and means of the processing of personal data. Where the purposes and means of processing are determined by national or Community laws or regulations, the controller or the specific criteria for his nomination may be designated by a national or Community law.

(e) "processor" shall mean the natural or legal person, public authority, agency or any other body which processes personal data on behalf of the controller;

(f) "third party" shall mean the natural or legal person, public authority, agency or any other body other than the data subject, the controller, the processor and the persons who, under the direct authority of the controller or the processor, are authorized to process the data;

(g) "recipient" shall mean the natural or legal person, public authority, agency or any other body to whom data are disclosed, whether a third party or not; however, authorities which may receive data in the framework of a particular inquiry shall not be regarded as recipients;

(h) "the data subject's consent" shall mean any freely given specific and informed indication of his wishes by which the data subject signifies his agreement to personal data relating to him being processed.

Article 3 Scope

1. This Directive shall apply to the processing of personal data wholly or partly by automatic means, and to the processing otherwise than by automatic means of personal data which form part of a filing system or are intended to form part of a filing system.

2. This Directive shall not apply to the processing of personal data:

-in the course of an activity which falls outside the scope of community law, such as those provided for by Titles V and VI of the Treaty on European Union and in any case to processing operations concerning public security, defence, State security (including the economic well-being of the State when the processing operation is bound up with questions of State security) and the activities of the State in areas of criminal law;

-by a natural person in the course of a purely personal or household activity.

Article 4 National law applicable

1. Each Member State shall apply the national provisions it adopts pursuant to this Directive to the processing of personal data where:

(a) the processing is carried out in the context of the activities of an establishment of the controller on the territory of the Member State; when the same controller is established on the territory of several Member States, he must take the necessary measures to ensure that each of these establishments complies with the obligations laid down by the national law applicable;

(b) the controller is not established on the Member State's territory, but in a place where its national law applies by virtue of international public law;

(c) the controller is not established on Community territory and, for purposes of processing personal data makes use of equipment, automated or otherwise, situated on the territory of said Member State, unless such equipment is used only for purposes of transit through the territory of the Community.

2. In the circumstances referred to in paragraph 1(c), the controller must designate a representative established in the territory of that Member State, without prejudice to legal actions which could be initiated against the controller himself.

Chapter II

General Rrules on the Lawfulness of the Processing of Personal Data

Article 5

Member States shall, within the limits of the provisions of this Chapter, determine more precisely the conditions under which the processing of personal data is lawful.

SECTION 1

PRINCIPLES RELATING TO DATA QUALITY

Article 6

1. Member States shall provide that personal data must be:
(a) processed fairly and lawfully;
(b) collected for specified, explicit and legitimate purposes and not further processed in a way incompatible with those purposes. Further processing of data for historical, statistical or scientific purposes shall not be considered as incompatible provided that Member States provide appropriate safeguards;
(c) adequate, relevant and not excessive in relation to the purposes for which they are collected and/or for which they are further processed;

(d) accurate and, where necessary, kept up to date; every reasonable step must be taken to ensure that data which are inaccurate or incomplete, having regard to the purposes for which they were collected or for which they are further processed, are erased or rectified;

(e) kept in a form which permits identification of data subjects for no longer that is necessary for the purposes for which the data were collected or for which they are further processed. Member Sates shall lay down appropriate safeguards for personal data stored for longer periods for historical, statistical or scientific use.

2. It shall be for the controller ro ensure that paragraph 1 is complied with.

SECTION II

PRINCIPLES RELATING TO THE REASONS FOR MAKING DATA PROCESSING LEGITIMATE

Article 7

Member States shall provide that personal data may be processed only if:

(a) the data subject has given his consent unambiguously;

or

(b) processing is necessary for the performance of a contact to which the data subject is party or in order to take steps at the request of the data subject entering into a contract.;

or

(c) processing is necessary for compliance with a legal obligation to which the controller is subject;

or

(d) processing is necessary in order to protect the vital interests of the data subject;

or

(e) processing is necessary for the performance of a task carried out in the public interest or in the exercise of official authority vested in the controller or in a third party to whom the data are disclosed;

or

(f) processing is necessary for the purposes of the legitimate interests pursued by the controller or by the third party or parties to whom the data are disclosed, except where such interests are overridden by the interests or fundamental rights and freedoms of the data subject which require protection under Article 1(1).

SECTION III

SPECIAL CATEGORIES OF PROCESSING

Article 8 The processing of special categories of data

1. Member States shall prohibit the processing of personal data revealing racial or ethnic origin, political opinions, religious or philosophical beliefs, trade-union membership, and the processing of data concerning health or sex life.
2. Paragraph 1 shall not apply where:
(a) the data subject has given his explicit consent to the processing of those data, except where the laws of the Member State provide that the prohibition referred to in paragraph 1 may not be waived by the data subject giving his consent.; or
(b) processing is necessary for the purposes of carrying out the obligations and specific rights of the controller in the field of employment law insofar as it is authorized by national law providing for adequate safeguards; or

(c) processing is necessary to protect the vital interests of the data subject or of another person where the data subject is physically or legally incapable of giving his consent; or

(d) processing is carried out in the course of its legitimate activities with appropriate guarantees by a foundation, association or any other non-profit-seeking body with a political, philosophical, religious or trade-union aim and on condition that the processing relates solely to the members of the body or to persons who have regular contact with it in connection with its purposes and that the data are not disclosed to a third party without the consent of the data subjects; or

(e) the processing relates to data which are manifestly made public by the data subject or is necessary for the establishment, exercise or defense of legal claims.

3. Paragraph 1 shall not apply where processing of the data is required for the purposes of preventive medicine, medical diagnosis, the provision of care or treatment or the management of health-care services, and where those data are processed by a health professional subject under national law or rules established by national competent bodies to the obligation of professional secrecy or by another person also subject to an equivalent obligation of secrecy.

4. Subject to the provision of suitable safeguards, Member States may lay down for reasons of important public interest, exemptions in addition to those laid down in paragraph 2 either by national law or by decision of the supervisory authority.

5. Processing of data relating to offences, criminal convictions or security measures may be carried out only under the control of official authority, or if suitable specific safeguards are provided under national law, subject to derogations which may be granted by the Member State under national provisions providing suitable

specific safeguards. However, a complete register of criminal convictions may be kept only under the control of official authority.

Member States may provide that data relating to administrative sanctions or civil trials shall also be processed under the control of official authority.

6. Derogations from paragraph 1 provided for in paragraphs 4 and 5 shall be notified to the Commission.

7. Member States shall determine the conditions under which a national identification number or any other identifier of general application may be processed.

Article 9 Processing of personal data and freedom of expression

Member States shall provide for exemptions or derogations from the provisions of this Chapter, Chapter IV and Chapter VI for the processing of personal data carried out solely for journalistic purposes or the purpose of artistic or literary expression only if they are necessary to reconcile the right to privacy with the rules governing freedom of expression.

Section IV

INFORMATION TO BE GIVEN TO THE DATA SUBJECT

Article 10 Information in cases of collection of data from the data subject

Member States shall provide that the controller or his representative must provide a data subject from whom data relating to himself are collected with at least the following information, except where he already knows:

(a) the identity of the controller and of his representative, if any,

(b) the purposes of the processing for which the data are intended,

(c) any further information such as

-the recipients or categories of recipients of the data;

-whether replies to the questions are obligatory or voluntary, as well as the possible consequences of the failure to reply;

-the existence of the right of access to and the right to rectify the data concerning him

insofar as they are necessary, having regard to the specific circumstances in which the data are collected, to guarantee fair processing in respect of the data subject.

Article 11 Information where the data have not been obtained from the data subject

1. Where the data have not been obtained from the data subject, Member States shall provide that the controller or his representative must at the time of undertaking the recording of personal data or if a disclosure to a third party is envisaged, no later than the time when the data are first disclosed provide the data subject with at least the following information, except where he already knows:

(a) the identity of the controller and of his representative, if any,

(b) the purposes of the processing,

(c) any further information such as

-the categories of data concerned

-the recipients or categories of recipients;

-the existence of the right of access to and the right to rectify the data concerning him

insofar as they are necessary, having regard to the specific circumstances in which the data are processed, to guarantee fair processing in respect of the data subject.

2. Paragraph 1 shall not apply where, in particular for processing for statistical purposes or for the purposes of historical or scientific research, the provision of information proves impossible or involves a disproportionate effort or if recording or disclosure is expressly laid down by law. In these cases Member States shall provide appropriate safeguards.

SECTION V

THE DATA SUBJECT'S RIGHT OF ACCESS TO DATA

Article 12 Right of access

Member States shall guarantee for every data subject the right to obtain from the controller:

1. without constraint at reasonable intervals and without excessive delay or expense:

-confirmation as to whether or not data relating to him are processed and information at least as to the purposes of the processing, the categories of data concerned, and the recipients or categories of recipients to whom the data are disclosed;

-communication to him in an intelligible form of the data undergoing processing and of any available information as to their source;

-knowledge of the logic involved in any automatic processing of data concerning him at least in the case of the automated decisions referred to in Article 15(1);

2. as appropriate the rectification, erasure or blocking of data, the processing of which does not comply with the provisions of this Directive, in particular because of the incomplete or inaccurate nature of the data;

3. notification to third parties to whom the data have been disclosed of any rectification, erasure or blocking carried out in compliance

with paragraph 2, unless this proves impossible or involves a disproportionate effort.

SECTION VI

EXEMPTIONS AND RESTRICTIONS

Article 13 Exemptions and restrictions

1. Member States may adopt legislative measures to restrict the scope
   of the obligations and rights provided for in Articles 6(1), 10,
   11(1), 12 and 21 when such a restriction constitutes a necessary
   measure to safeguard:
   (a) national security;
   (b) defence;
   (c) public security;
   (d) the prevention, investigation, detection and prosecution of crim-
       inal offences, or of breaches of ethics for regulated professions;
   (e) an important economic or financial interest of a Member State or
       of the European Union, including monetary, budgetary and taxa-
       tion matters;
   (f) a monitoring, inspection or regulatory function connected, even
       occasionally, with the exercise of official authority in cases
       referred to in (c), (d) and (e);
   (g) the protection of the data subject or of the rights and freedoms of
       others.
2. Subject to adequate legal guarantees, in particular that the data are
   not used for taking measures or decisions regarding any particular
   individual data subject, Member States may restrict, by a legislative
   measure, the rights provided for in Article 12 when data are
   processed solely for purposes of scientific research or are kept in

personal form for a period which does not exceed the period necessary for the sole purpose of creating statistics.

SECTION VII

THE DATA SUBJECT'S RIGHT TO OBJECT

Article 14 The data subject's right to object

Member States shall grant the data subject the right:

(a) at least in the cases referred to in Article 7(e) and (f), to object at any time on compelling legitimate grounds relating to his particular situation to the processing of data relating to him, save where otherwise provided by national legislation. Where there is a justified objection, the processing instigated by the controller may no longer involve those data;

(b) to object, on request and free of charge, to the processing of personal data relating to him which the controller anticipates being processed for the purposes of direct marketing;

or

to be informed before personal data are disclosed for the first time to third parties or used on their behalf for the purposes of direct marketing, and to be expressly offered the right to object free of charge to such disclosures or uses.

Member States shall take the necessary measures to ensure that data subjects are aware of the existence of the right referred to in the first subparagraph of (b).

Article 15 Automated individual decisions

1. Member States shall grant the right to every person not to be subject to a decision which produces legal effects concerning him or

significantly affects him and which is based solely on automated processing of data intended to evaluate certain personal aspects relating to him, such as his performance at work, creditworthiness, reliability, conduct, etc.

2. Subject to the other Articles of this Directive, Member States shall provide that a person may be subjected to a decision of the kind referred to in paragraph 1 if that decision:

(a) is taken in the course of entering into or performance of a contract, provided the request by the data subject has been satisfied, or that there are suitable measures to safeguard his legitimate interests, such as arrangements allowing him to defend his point of view; or

(b) is authorized by a law which also lays down measures to safeguard the data subject's legitimate interests.

SECTION VIII

CONFIDENTIALITY AND SECURITY OF PROCESSING

Article 16 Confidentiality of processing

Any person acting under the authority of the controller or of the processor, including the processor himself, who has access to personal data must not process them except on instructions from the controller, unless he is required to do so by law.

Article 17 Security of processing

1. Member States shall provide that the controller must implement appropriate technical and organizational measures to protect personal data against accidental or unlawful destruction or accidental loss and against unauthorized alteration, disclosure or access, in

particular where the processing involves the transmission of data over a network, and against all other unlawful forms of processing. Having regard to the state of the art and the costs of their implementation, such measures shall ensure a level of security appropriate to the risks represented by the processing and the nature of the data to be protected.

2. The Member States shall provide that the controller must, where processing is carried out on his behalf, choose a processor who provides sufficient guarantees in respect of the technical security measures and organizational measures governing the processing to be carried out and must ensure compliance with those measures.

3. The carrying out of processing by way of a processor must be governed by a contract or legal act binding the processor to the controller and stipulating in particular that:

-the processor shall act only on instructions from the controller;

-the obligations set out in paragraph 1, as defined by the law of the Member State in which the processor is established, shall also be incumbent on the processor.

4. For the purposes of keeping proof, the parts of the contract or legal act relating to data protection and the requirements relating to the measures referred to in paragraph 1 shall be in writing or in another equivalent form.

SECTION IX

NOTIFICATION

Article 18 Obligation to notify the supervisory authority

1. Member States shall provide that the controller or his representative, if any, must notify the supervisory authority referred to in Article 28 before carrying out any wholly or partly automatic processing

operation or set of such operations intended to serve a single purpose or several related purposes.

    2. Member States may provide for the simplification of or exemption from notification only in the following cases and under the following conditions:

-where, for categories of processing operations which are unlikely, taking account of the data to be processed, to affect adversely the rights and freedoms of data subjects, they specify the purposes of the processing, the data or categories of data undergoing processing, the category or categories of data subject, the recipients or categories of recipient to whom the data are to be disclosed and the length of time the data are to be stored and/or

-where the controller appoints, in compliance with the national law which governs him, a data protection official, responsible in particular

=for ensuring in an independent manner the internal application of the national provisions taken pursuant to this Directive

=for keeping the register of processing operations carried out by the controller, containing the items of information referred to in Article 21(2),

thereby ensuring that the rights and freedoms of the data subjects are unlikely to be adversely affected by the processing operations.

    3. Member States may provide that paragraph 1 does not apply to processing whose sole purpose is the keeping of a register, which according to laws or regulations is intended to provide information to the public and which is open to consultation either by the public in general or by any person demonstrating a legitimate interest.

    4. Member States may provide for an exemption from the obligation to notify or a simplification of the notification in the case or processing operations referred to in Article 8(2)(d).

    5. Member States may stipulate that certain or all non-automatic processing operations involving personal data shall be notified, or

provide for these processing operations to be subject to a simplified notification.

Article 19 Contents of notification

1. Member States shall specify the information to be given in the notification. It shall include at least:
(a) the name and address of the controller and of his representative, if any;
(b) the purpose or purposes of the processing;
(c) a description of the category or categories of data subject and of the data or categories of data relating to them;
(d) the recipients or categories of recipient to whom the data might be disclosed;
(e) proposed transfers of data to third countries;
(f) a general description allowing a preliminary assessment to be made of the appropriateness of the measures taken pursuant to Article 17 to ensure security of processing.
2. Member States shall specify the procedures under which any change affecting the information referred to in paragraph 1 must be notified to the supervisory authority.

Article 20 Prior checking

1. States shall determine the processing operations likely to present specific risks for the rights and freedoms of data subjects and shall check that these processing operations are examined prior to the start thereof.
2. Such prior checks shall be carried out by the supervisory authority following receipt of a notification from the controller or by the data protection official, who in cases of doubt must consult the supervisory authority.

3. Member States may also carry out such checks in the context of preparation of a measure (?) decided on by the national parliament or based on such a decision, defining the nature of the processing operation and laying down appropriate safeguards.

Article 21 Publicizing of processing operations

1. Member States shall take measures to ensure that processing operations are publicized.
2. Member States shall provide that a register of processing operations notified in accordance with Article 18 shall be kept by the supervisory authority.

The register shall contain at least the information listed in Article 19(1)(a) to (e).

The register may be inspected by any person.

3. Member States shall provide, in relation to processing operations not subject to notification, that controllers or another body appointed by the Member States make available at least the information referred to in Article 19(1)(a) to (e) in an appropriate fashion to any person on request.

Member States may provide that this provision does not apply to processing whose sole purpose is the keeping of a register, which according to laws or regulations is intended to provide information to the public and which is open to consultation either by the public in general or by any person who can provide proof of a legitimate interest.

CHAPTER III

JUDICIAL REMEDIES, LIABILITY AND PENALTIES

Article 22 Remedies

Without prejudice to any administrative remedy for which provision may be made, inter alia before the supervisory authority referred to in Article 28, prior to referral to the judicial authority, Member States shall provide for the right of every person to a judicial remedy for any breach of the rights guaranteed him by the national law applicable to the processing in question.

Article 23 Liability

1. Member States shall provide that any person who has suffered damage as a result of an unlawful processing operation or of any act incompatible with the national provisions adopted pursuant to this Directive is entitled to receive compensation from the controller for the damage suffered.
2. The controller may be exempted from this liability, in whole or in part, if he proves that he is not responsible for the event giving rise to the damage.

Article 24 Sanctions

The Member States shall adopt suitable measures to ensure the full implementation of the provisions of this Directive and shall in particular lay down the sanctions to be imposed in case of infringement of the provisions adopted pursuant to this Directive.

CHAPTER IV

TRANSFER OF PERSONAL DATA TO THIRD COUNTRIES

Article 25 Principles

1. Member States shall provide that the transfer to a third country of personal data which are undergoing processing or are intended for processing after transfer may take place only if, without prejudice to compliance with the national provisions adopted pursuant to the other provisions of this Directive, the third country in question ensures an adequate level of protection.

2. The adequacy of the level of protection afforded by a third country shall be assessed in the light of all the circumstances surrounding a data transfer operation or set of data transfer operations; particular consideration shall be given to the nature of the data, the purpose and duration of the proposed processing operation or operations, the country of origin and country of final destination, the rules of law, both general and sectoral, in force in the third country in question and the professional rules and security measures which are complied with in those countries.

3. ember States and the Commission shall inform each other of cases where the consider that a third country does not ensure an adequate level of protection within the meaning of paragraph 2.

4. Where the Commission finds, under the procedure provided for in Article 31(2), that a third country does not ensure an adequate level of protection within the meaning of paragraph 2 of

this Article Member States shall take the measures necessary to prevent the transfer of data of the same type to the third country in question.

5. At the appropriate time, the Commission shall enter into negotiations with a view to remedying the situation resulting from the funding made pursuant to paragraph 4.

6. The Commission may find, in accordance with the procedure referred to in Article 31(2), that a third country ensures an adequate level of protection within the meaning of paragraph 2 of this Article, by reason of its domestic law or of the international commitments it has entered into, particularly upon conclusion of the negotiations referred to in paragraph 5, for the protection of the private lives and basic freedoms and rights of individuals.

Member States shall take the measures necessary to comply with the Commission's decision.

Article 26 Derogations

1. By way of derogation from Article 25 and save where otherwise provided by domestic law governing particular cases, Member States shall provide that a transfer or a set of transfers of personal data to a third country which does not ensure an adequate level of protection within the meaning of Article 25(2) may take place on condition that:

1) the data subject has given his consent unambiguously to the proposed transfer, or

2) the transfer is necessary for the performance of a contract between the data subject and the controller or the implementation of precontractual measures taken in response to the data subject's request, or

3) the transfer is necessary for the conclusion or for the performance of a contract concluded in the interest of the data subject between the controller and a third party, or

4) the transfer is necessary or legally required on important public interest grounds, or for the establishment, exercise or defence of legal claims, or

5) the transfer is necessary in order to protect the vital interests of the data subject, or

6) the transfer is made from a register which according to laws or regulations is intended to provide information to the public and which is open to consultation either by the public in general or by any person who can demonstrate legitimate interest, to the extent that the conditions laid down in law for consultation are fulfilled in the particular case.

2. Without prejudice to paragraph 1, a Member State may authorize a transfer or a set of transfers of personal data to a third country which does not ensure an adequate level of protection within the meaning of Article 25(2), where the controller adduces sufficient guarantees with respect to the protection of the privacy and fundamental rights and freedoms of individuals and as regards the exercise of the corresponding rights; such guarantees may in particular result from appropriate contractual clauses.

3. The Member State shall inform the Commission and the other Member States of the authorizations granted pursuant to paragraph 2.

If a Member State or the Commission objects on justified grounds involving the protection of the privacy and fundamental rights and freedoms of individuals, the Commission shall take appropriate measures in accordance with the procedure laid down in Article 31(2).

Member States shall take the necessary measures to comply with the Commission's decision.

4. Where the Commission decides, in accordance with the procedure referred to in Article 31(2), that certain standard contractual clauses offer sufficient guarantees required by paragraph 2, Member States shall take the necessary measures to comply with the Commission's decision.

CHAPTER V

CODES OF CONDUCT

Article 27

1. The Member States and the Commission shall encourage the drawing up of codes of conduct intended to contribute to the proper implementation of the national provisions adopted by the Member States pursuant to this Directive, taking account of the specific features of the various sectors.

2. Member States shall make provision for trade associations and other bodies representing other categories of controllers which have drawn up draft national codes or which have the intention of amending or extending existing national codes to be able to submit them to the opinion of the national authority.

Member States shall make provision for this authority to ascertain, among other things, whether the drafts submitted to it are in accordance with the national provisions adopted pursuant to this Directive. If it sees fit, the authority shall seek the views of data subjects or their representatives.

3. Draft Community codes, and amendments or extensions to existing Community codes, may be submitted to the Working Party referred to in Article 29. This Working Party shall determine, among other things, whether the drafts submitted to it are in accordance with the national provisions adopted pursuant to this Directive. If it sees fit, the authority shall seek the views of data subjects or their representatives. The Commission may ensure

appropriate publicity for the codes which have been approved by the Working Party.

Chapter VI

Supervisory Authority and Working Party on the Protection of Individuals with Regard to the Processing of Personal Data

Article 28 Supervisory authority

1. Each Member State shall provide that one or more public authorities are responsible for monitoring the application within its territory of the provisions adopted by the Member States pursuant to this Directive.

These authorities shall act with complete independence in exercising the functions entrusted to them.

2. Each Member State shall provide that the supervisory authorities are consulted when drawing up administrative measures or regulations relating to the protection of individuals' rights and freedoms with regard to the processing of personal data.

3. Each authority shall in particular be endowed with:

-investigative powers, such as powers of access to data forming the subject-matter of processing operations and powers to collect all the information necessary for the performance of its supervisory duties;

-effective powers of intervention, such as, for example, that of delivering opinions in accordance with Article 20, before processing operations are carried out and ensuring appropriate publication of such opinions, or that of ordering the blocking, erasure or destruction of data, or of imposing a temporary or definitive ban on processing, or that of warning or admonishing the controller or that of referring the matter to national parliaments or other political institutions;

-the power to engage in legal proceedings where the national provisions adopted pursuant to this Directive have been violated or to bring these violations to the attention of the judicial authorities.

Decisions by the supervisory authority which give rise to complaints may be appealed against through the courts.

4. Each supervisory authority shall hear claims lodged by any person, or by an association representing that person, concerning the protection of his rights and freedoms in regard to the processing of personal data. The person concerned shall be informed of the outcome of the claim.

Each supervisory authority shall, in particular, hear claims for checks on the lawfulness of data processing lodged by any person when the national provisions adopted pursuant to Article 13 of this Directive apply. The person shall at any rate be informed that a check has taken place.

5. Each supervisory authority shall draw up a report on its activities at regular intervals. The report shall be made public.

6. Each supervisory authority is competent, whatever the national law applicable to the processing in question, for exercising, on the territory of its own Member State, the powers attributed to it in accordance with paragraph 3. Each authority may be requested to exercise its powers by an authority of another Member State.

The supervisory authorities shall cooperate with one another to the extent necessary for the performance of their duties, in particular by exchanging all useful information.

7. Member States shall provide that the members and staff of the supervisory authority, even after their employment has ended,

are to be subject to a duty of professional secrecy with regard to confidential information to which they have access.

Article 29 Working Party on the Protection of Individuals with regard to the Processing of Personal Data

1. A Working Party on the Protection of Individuals with regard to the Processing of Personal Data, hereinafter referred to as "the Working Party", is hereby set up.

It shall have advisory status and act independently.

2. The Working Party shall be composed of a representative of the supervisory authority or authorities designated by each Member State and of a representative of the authority or authorities established for Community institutions and bodies, and of a representative of the Commission.

Each member of the Working Party shall be designated by the institution, authority or authorities which he represents. Where a Member State designates more than one supervisory authority, they shall nominate a joint representative. The same shall apply for the authorities established for Community institutions and bodies.

3. The Working Party shall take decisions by a simple majority of the representatives of the supervisory authorities.

4. The Working Party shall elect its chairman. The chairman's term of office shall be two years. His appointment shall be renewable.

5. The Working Party's secretariat shall be provided by the Commission.

6. The Working Party shall adopt its own rules of procedure.

7. The Working Party shall consider items placed on its agenda by its chairman, either on his own initiative or at the request of a representative of the supervisory authorities or at the Commission's request.

Article 30

1. The Working Party shall:

(a) examine any question covering the application of the national measures adopted under this Directive in order to contribute to the uniform application of such measures;

(b) give the Commission an opinion on the level of protection in the Community and in third countries;

(c) advise the Commission on any proposed amendment of this Directive, on any additional or specific measures to safeguard the rights and freedoms of natural persons with regard to the processing of personal data and on any other proposed Community measures affecting such rights and freedoms;

(d) give an opinion on codes of conduct drawn up at Community level.

2. If the Working Party finds that divergences likely to affect the equivalence of protection for persons with regard to the processing of personal data in the Community are arising between the laws or practices of Member States, it shall inform the Commission accordingly.

3. Working Party may, on its own initiative, make recommendations on all matters relating to the protection of persons with regard to the processing of personal data in the Community.

4. The Working Party's opinions and recommendations shall be forwarded to the Commission and to the committee referred to in Article 31.

5. The Commission shall inform the Working Party of the action it has taken in response to its opinions and recommendations. It shall do so in a report which shall also be forwarded to the European Parliament and the Council. The report shall be made public.

6. The Working Party shall draw up an annual report on the situation regarding the protection of natural persons with regard to the processing of personal data in the Community and in third countries,

which it shall transmit to the Commission, the European Parliament and the Council. The report shall be made public.

CHAPTER VII

COMMUNITY IMPLEMENTING MEASURES

Article 31 The Committee

1. The Commission shall be assisted by a committee composed of the representatives of the Member States and chaired by the representative of the Commission.

2. The representative of the Commission shall submit to the committee a draft of the measures to be taken. The committee shall deliver its opinion on the draft within a time limit which the chairman may lay down according to the urgency of the matter.

The opinion shall be delivered by the majority laid down in Article 148(2) of the Treaty. The votes of the representatives of the Member States within the committee shall be weighted in the manner set out in that Article. The chairman shall not vote.

The Commission shall adopt measures which shall apply immediately. However, if these measures are not in accordance with the opinion of the committee, they shall be communicated by the Commission to the Council forthwith. In that event:

The Commission shall defer application of the measures which it has decided for a period to be laid down in each act adopted by the Council, but which may in on case exceed three months from the date of communication.

The Council, acting by a qualified majority, may take a different decision within the time limit referred to in the previous paragraph.

FINAL PROVISIONS

Article 32

1. Member States shall bring into force the laws, regulations and administrative provisions necessary to comply with this Directive at the latest at the end of a period of three years from the adoption of the Directive.

When Member States adopt these measures, they shall contain a reference to this Directive or be accompanied by such reference on the occasion of their official publication. The methods of making such reference shall be laid down by the Member States.

2. States shall ensure that processing already underway on the date the national provisions adopted pursuant to this Directive enter into force, is brought into conformity with these provisions within 3 years of this date.

By way of derogation from the preceding subparagraph, Member States may provide that the processing of data already held in manual filing systems on the date of entry into force of the national provisions adopted in implementation of this Directive shall be brought into conformity with Articles 6,7 and 8 within 12 years of the date on which this Directive is adopted. Member States shall, however, grant the data subject the right to obtain, at his request and in particular at the time of exercising his right of access, the rectification, erasure or blocking of data which are incomplete, inaccurate or stored in a way incompatible with the legitimate purposes pursued by the controller.

3. By way of derogation from paragraph 2, Member States may provide, subject to suitable safeguards, that data kept for the sole purpose of historical research are not brought into conformity with Articles 6,7 and 8 of this Directive.

4. Member States shall communicate to the Commission the provisions of national law which they adopt in the field covered by this Directive.

Article 33

The Commission shall report to the Council and the European Parliament at regular intervals, starting not later than three years after the date referred to in Article 32(1), on the implementation of this Directive, attaching to its report, if necessary, suitable proposals for amendments. The report shall be made public.

The Commission shall examine, in particular, the application of this Directive to the data processing of sound and image data relating to natural persons and shall submit any appropriate proposals which prove to be necessary, taking account of developments in information technology and in the light of the state of progress in the information society.

Article 34

This Directive is addressed to the Member States
Done at Brussels,
For the European Parliament For the Council
The President The President

Bibliography

Baker, Richard, Bereuter, Doug, and McCollum, Bill, United States House of Representatives Banking Finance, and Urban Affairs Committee, "Joint Letter to Acting Comptroller of the Currency, Julie Williams", October 26, 1998.

Baxter, John D. State Security, Privacy and Information. 1990.

Bonavia, Marjorie I., Morton, Lois Wright. Personal Information Privacy Issues Relating to Consumption in the U.S. Marketplace. Consumer Interests Annual, volume 44, 1998.

Brill, Alida. Nobody's Business: The Paradoxes of Privacy. 1990.

Brill, Allan. The Right To Financial Privacy Act: A Compliance Guide For Financial Institutions. Prentice-Hall, 1998.

Cate, Fred H. Privacy in the Information Age. 1997.

Campbell, Dennis, Fisher, Joy ed. Data Transmission and Privacy, 1994.

"CDT Analysis of the Federal Trade Commission Report on Online", Center for Democracy and Technology, www.cdt.org.

Clarke, Linda, ed. "Confidentiality and the Law", 1990.

Clark, Robert. "Data protection law in Ireland".

Confidentiality, Privacy a Selected Bibliography: The Privacy Act of 1974 Volume One.

Cooper, Jonathan, ed. "Liberating Cyberspace: Civil Liberties, Human Rights, and the Internet", 1998.

Data protection legislation: an Internet. documentation: English. - German = Die Gesetzgebung zum Datenschutz.

Diffie, Whitfield; Landau, Susan. Privacy on the Line: The Politics of Wiretapping and Encryption. 1998.

Dill, Barbara. "The Journalist's Handbook on Libel and Privacy", 1986.

"An Exploration of Legal Issues in Information and Communication Technologies", Information, Computer, Communication Policy, 1984.

Directive 95/46/EC of the European Parliament and of the Council of the Protection of Individuals with Regard to the Processing of Personal Data and the Free Movement, October 24, 1995.

"Electronic Bill of Rights", The White House, Office of the Vice President July 31, 1998.

"Elements of Effective Self Regulation for Protection of Privacy", National Telecommunications and Information Administration, United States Department of Commerce, June 5, 1998.

Equifax-Harris. Consumer Privacy Survey. New York: Louis Harris and Associates, October 8, 1996.

"European Commission Adopts Directive On Protection Of Personal Data"
European Commission Press Release: IP/95/822, July 25, 1995.

"European Union Data Commission's Working Document on transfers of personal data to third countries, October 1998."

The Fair Credit Reporting Act: hearing before the Subcommittee on Consumer and Regulatory Affairs of the Committee on Banking, Housing, and Urban Affairs, United States Senate, One Hundred Second Congress, first session, on consumer groups and others who argue that the current law is ineffective with problems of inaccuracy, consumer privacy, and not keeping pace with technological developments in the industry, October 22, 1991.

Federal Deposit Insurance Corporation, "Online Privacy of Consumer Personal Information", August 17, 1998.

"Federal Deposit Insurance Corporation" Web site, December 1998.

"Financial Privacy In America, A Review of Consumer Financial Services Issues", June, 1998.

Flaherty, David H. "Privacy and Government Data Banks: An International Perspective". 1979.

Franklin, Charles E.H., ed. "Business Guide to Privacy and Data Protection Legislation", ICC Publication 498, International Chamber 1995.

Franklin, Justin D; Bouchard, Robert F. ed. "Guidebook to the Freedom of Information and Privacy Acts", 1986.

Gelman, Robert B, et al. Protecting Yourself Online: The Definitive Resource on Safety, Freedom, and Privacy in Cyberspace. 1988.

Godwin, Mike; Smith, T, ed. Cyber Rights: Privacy and Free Speech in the Digital Age. 1998.

"Guidelines on the protection of privacy and transborder flows of personal data".

Hondius, Frits W. "Emerging data protection in Europe".

"Intellectual Property and Technology Law Letter", Morgan, Lewis, & Bockius, volume 6, number 7, September 1998.

Kahin, Brian; Nesson, Charles, eds. Borders in Cyberspace: Information Policy and the Global Information Infrastructure (publication of the Harvard Information Infrastructure Project), 1997.

Louis Harris & Associates, Westin, Allan F. "Privacy Concerns & Consumer Choice: A Privacy and American Business Survey", November 18, 1998.

Michael, James "Privacy and Human Rights: An International and Comparative Study, With Special Reference to Developments in Information Technology", 1994.

Nugter, A. "Transborder Flow of Personal Data Within the EC: A Comparative Analysis of Princiepstat", 1991.

Office of the Comptroller of the Currency, "Bulletin 98-33", August 3, 1998.

"Office of the Comptroller of the Currency" Web site, November 1998.
Office of Thrift Supervision, "Policy Statement on Privacy and Accuracy of Personal Customer Information", November 3, 1998.

"Office of Thrift Supervision" Web site, December 1998.
Privacy Act 1993: a selection of background materials on the Privacy Act 1993 and the Office of the Privacy Commissioner, July 1992-April 1994.

Privacy and the Canadian information highway.

"Privacy and Data Protection: Issues and Challenges", OECD Documents, 1994.
"Privacy and Human Rights", 1994.

"Records, Computers and the Rights of Citizens", United States Department of Health, Education, and Welfare's, 1973.

Reidenberg, Joel R, Schwartz, Paul M. Data Privacy Law. 1996.

Servais, Jean-Michel, "Inviolability of trade union premises and communications".

"Safe Harbor Letter", Undersecretary David L. Aaron, United States Department of Commerce, November 4, 1998.

Sizer, Richard; Newman, Philip. Data Protection Act : A Practical Guide. 1984.

U.S. Federal Trade Commission (FTC), 1998, Privacy Online: A Report to Congress. Washington: Federal Trade Commission Bureau of Consumer Protection. Available at http://www.ftc.gov.

Wacks, Raymond. "Personal Information: Privacy and the Law", 1994.

White, Anthony, "Confidentiality Privacy Issues: A Bibliographic Update (P2146)", 1987.

"Working Document: Preliminary views on the use of contractual provisions in the context of transfers of personal data to third countries", Working Party on the Protection of Individuals with regard to the Processing of Personal Data, April 22, 1998.

Yankelovich Partners, "Balancing the Power of Information with Consumer Privacy", 1994.

ABOUT THE AUTHOR

Dr. Benjamin E. Robinson III is the vice president of public affairs for MasterCard International and a registered lobbyist. In addition, Dr. Robinson is the chief policy advisor for TDS Corporation, a MasterCard subsidiary. He manages international public policy, government relations, economic analysis, and thought leadership platforms. His responsibilities include government affairs, and issue management, as well as regulatory affairs for MasterCard's Global Chip and Electronic Commerce divisions; Mondex™, its chip-based electronic cash program; and MULTOS™, MasterCard's smart card operating system. An author of numerous papers and articles on the banking industry, Dr. Robinson is internationally recognized in his field. In addition, he serves on the faculty of the Hagan School of Business at Iona College in Westchester County, N.Y.

In 1993, Dr. Robinson was appointed to the U.S. House of Representatives Subcommittee on Consumer Credit & Insurance. As a congressional advisor to the committee, he advised former Congressman Joseph P. Kennedy II on banking issues affecting the United States. Prior to the United States House of Representatives, Dr. Robinson held positions with Mellon Bank as a senior cash management officer and Fleet Bank as a corporate banking officer.

Dr. Robinson received a Bachelor of Arts from Bates College, where he was a Benjamin Mays Scholar. He holds a Master of Arts in public policy from Trinity College and a Doctor of Philosophy in banking and finance policy from The Union Graduate School.

Dr. Robinson is married to Cecilia Atkinson of Lorain, Ohio and resides in Connecticut. They have two children.

www.ingramcontent.com/pod-product-compliance
Lightning Source LLC
Chambersburg PA
CBHW030803180526
45163CB00003B/1145